A SHEPHERD'S LETTER

The Faith Once and For All Delivered to the Evangelical Church

A SHEPHERD'S LETTER

The Faith Once and For All Delivered to the Evangelical Church

BO GIERTZ

TRANSLATED BY BROR ERICKSON

A Shepherd's Letter: The Faith Once and For All Delivered to the Evangelical Church

Published by:
1517 Publishing
PO Box 54032
Irvine, CA 92619-4032

Publisher's Cataloging-In-Publication Data
(Prepared by The Donohue Group, Inc.)

Names: Giertz, Bo, 1905-1998, author. | Erickson, Bror, translator.
Title: A shepherd's letter : the faith once and for all delivered to the Evangelical Church / by Bo Giertz ; translated by Bror Erickson.
Other Titles: Herdabrev till prästerskapet och församlingarna i Göteborgs stift. English
Description: Irvine, CA : 1517 Publishing, [2022] | Translation of: Herdabrev till prästerskapet och församlingarna i Göteborgs stift. Stockholm : Svenska Kyrkans Diakonistyrelses Bokförlag, 1949.
Identifiers: ISBN 9781948969987 (paperback) | ISBN 9781948969994 (ebook)
Subjects: LCSH: Svenska kyrkan—Pastoral letters and charges. | Lutheran Church—Sweden—Göteborg—Pastoral letters and charges. | Lutheran Church—Bishops—Correspondence. | LCGFT: Pastoral letters and charges.
Classification: LCC BX8040.G6 G5413 2022 (print) | LCC BX8040.G6 (ebook) | DDC 284.1485—dc23

Printed in the United States of America.

Cover art by Zachariah James Stuef.

CONTENTS

TRANSLATOR'S PREFACE

"A Shepherd's Letter; The Faith Once and For All Delivered to the Evangelical Church" Is a translation of "Herdabrev Till Göteborgs Stift." Literally translated this is "A Shepherd's Letter to the Gothenburg Diocese." It is somewhat a tradition in Sweden for bishops to write books introducing themselves and explaining their agenda for the diocese upon election. These are often rushed affairs and Bo Giertz also complained that he did not have more time to put this book together. However, it was recognized rather early that what Bishop Giertz had to say to his own diocese had wider application and was translated within a few years as

"Sendschreiben an die evangelische Christen-heit." I used this title of the German translation as well as a Bible verse that was theologically programmatic for Giertz, Jude 3, as the subtitle for the English translation.

Bo Giertz was forty-four years old when he was elected Bishop of Gothenburg, a post he held until retirement in 1970. During this time there were many things to keep a bishop occupied and his literary output slowed to a trickle. Most of what he wrote after Herdabrev dealt more or less with administrative issues facing the church, Bishop's reports. Though his weekly pericope studies were collected and formed into "Preaching from the Whole Bible." In retirement he would write "The Knights of Rhodes" "To Live with Christ" and "New Testament Devotional Commentaries" as the books are known in English. Yet Jude 3 plays a prominent role in almost all of his writing before and after Herdabrev. Beloved, although I was very eager to write to you about our common salvation, I found it necessary to write appealing to you to contend for the faith that was once for all delivered to the saints."(Jude 3) "The faith... once for all delivered to the saints." It was this that Bishop Giertz would contend for, and this book is thorough going study of that faith.

Only one chapter of this book has previously been translated into English, "Liturgy and Spiritual Awakening." Clifford Ansgar Nelson translated this by itself and left the rest. This chapter can be found floating around various places on the internet and is well worth a read by everyone who has ever had to question what worship is about. As great as the essay is on its own, I think readers will understand how much more sense it makes in the context of this book.

Readers who have never read anything by Bo Giertz before will find this to be a great introduction into his theological mindset. Others who have perhaps read the "Hammer of God" or some other work of his will perhaps recognize different themes that Bo Giertz constantly returns to in his work. Here the cards are out on the table.

They help a person better understand and probe deeper into the prose of his other works.

Your Brother in Christ

Pastor Bror Erickson

Palm Sunday 2022

CRISES AND SOURCES OF STRENGTH

Blessed be the God and Father of our Lord Jesus Christ!
According to his great mercy, he has caused us to be born
again to a living hope through the resurrection of Jesus
Christ from the dead. (1 Peter 1:3)

I want to begin with this apostolic thanksgiving today when I greet you, fathers and brothers in the office, beloved fellow Christians of all ages and positions within the diocese of Gothenburg. The situation of the church is serious and the times are full of worries, and for just that reason I will begin by praising the God and Father of our Lord Jesus Christ for the living hope to which we have been given rebirth.

Some twenty years ago, Carl Elis Daniel Block was installed as bishop on Prayer Sunday. For twenty toil-filled years, he literally gave his life for his diocese. The congregations remember him as a zealous shepherd of souls who proclaimed the Word from the pulpit with a calm, persuasive power, or stood in the midst of the congregation to generously share what he had collected through prayer and toil from the treasure vaults of Scripture. I will not try to trace this image here. Others are better suited to do that. It is sufficient to say that with his tireless fidelity to the Confessions, his affection for souls, and his love for his diocese, Bishop Block left behind an inheritance that gives every single one of his successors a model to follow.

The twenty years between Prayer Sunday 1929 and the same Sunday in 1949 have been a restless and unfortunate period. Western lands have been shaken to their foundations. All the truths and values, without which a Christian culture cannot last, have been attacked by reckless forces. The church has suffered through harsh periods of persecution. The number of martyrs has increased by tens of thousands, and the number of those who live under daily threat to their lives and freedoms on account of their faith is greater than at any time during the church's two-thousand-year history. Even where, as with us, the church has been able to work comfortably in peace, the opposition has hardened. Unlike before when the sharpest attacks were directed at her teachings, they are now directed at the Christian way of life. The spirit is not merely critical of Christendom, but clearly hostile toward Christ. Some regard this Gospel as something evil, and aggressively and purposefully seek to exclude it from hospitals, schools, and social services. And finally: no one knows if tomorrow will also come for us with the sort of tests that we have been spared during the thousand years when the Gospel has been a decisive factor in Swedish culture, to the benefit of our people.

So, the situation is critical. Let us then remember that it was no less critical in the apostolic era. The letters of the apostle Peter, whose word I just cited, bear the traces of danger and suffering that were apparently fulfilled every day, not only for him but for each and every individual who dared to confess that Jesus Christ is Lord. Yet this letter is not a lamentation, but a great song of praise.

Early Christendom regarded persecution as something completely natural. To be slandered and lied to, to receive suffering in return for good deeds, to take a punch and be assaulted, these are only a natural part of the sufferings of Christ that are imposed upon us. "Beloved, do not be surprised at the fiery trial when it comes upon you to test you, as though something strange were happening to you. But rejoice insofar as you share Christ's sufferings, that you may also rejoice and be glad when his glory is revealed" (1 Peter 4:12–13).

So early Christendom did not quarrel. On the contrary: the suffering and the injustices were seen only as sharp shadows in the flood of sunlight. The New Testament is full of an irresistible joy, a jubilee that breaks forth from overflowing hearts. The Gospel is a joyous cry, trembling with zeal and happiness: We have seen it! We proclaim to you the Life, the eternal Life that was with the Father and revealed to us. We saw his glory! God raised him from the dead, so we too can witness! We have all received from his fullness. Everything comes from God who has reconciled us with himself through Jesus Christ. So, we are always glad. Blessed is God who has blessed us in Christ with all the spiritual blessings of the heavenly world!

This great joy is the keynote of early Christendom. It is joy over the unfathomable and overwhelming thing that has just now happened: the only begotten Son has dwelt among us. He has atoned for our sins. He has conquered death and been raised up from his grave. He has sent his lifegiving spirit and now proceeds in a victory parade through the world. The church rejoices over him with ineffable and glorious joy. Here the unexplored wealth is given for nothing. Here is the blessed mystery that had been hidden through the centuries but is now shouted from the rooftops.

Before this fact, everything else is small and meaningless. The resurrection witnesses did not sit down to calculate how a person might be expected to react or what they might be willing to hear. They knew very well that they were sent as sheep among wolves. They knew that they were disciples if they suffered their master's fate. They had heard from his own lips that they would be hated by all for his name's sake. However, they were witnesses to the resurrection. They had seen with their own eyes what God had done. They knew that Christ is right and that it is he and no one else that is set as Lord over the living and the dead. So, they went out singing praises and full of joy. And when it went so far that they were whipped and forbidden to speak in the name of Jesus, they went out and continued their preaching, "rejoicing that they were counted worthy to suffer dishonor for the name" (Acts 5:41).

Born again to a living hope through Jesus Christ's resurrection—this is the mystery of Christianity. This is what makes it invincible. This has its basis in a fact that no one can erase: Jesus is resurrected from the dead. So long as he lives, his church also lives. And he lives eternally.

This does not mean that the church lives a tranquil life in this world, quite the opposite. "In the world you will have tribulation. But take heart; I have overcome the world" (John 16:33). In the world the situation of the church is always critical and cannot be anything but critical. Even before the crises that shake her now, we had every reason to say to each other: "Beloved, do not be surprised . . . as though something strange were happening to you." The Gospel is something so unreasonable that it can never be accepted without opposition—unless it ceases to be gospel.

Even on her very first day, the situation of the church was unreasonable. Twelve men from the lower strata of society had the commission

to preach that Jesus was the Christ, that an exe-
cuted radical was God's Son and that he who
died helpless and abandoned before everyone's
eyes possessed all authority in Heaven and on
Earth. They would preach it in a city where he
had already been rejected, and before men who
had been there to cry, "Crucify him!" It was
clear to everyone from the very beginning that
the cause was hopeless.

And then it succeeded! All human calcula-
tions were put to shame. There was one factor
in the course of events that the world's politi-
cians and organizers did not count on. It was
the factor old Gamaliel asked the Sanhedrin to
consider in a momentary afterthought: if this is
of God, then you cannot defeat these men.

It is only possible to preach that an exe-
cuted prophet has triumphed over the dead if
he really has done it. It is only possible to go out
and make all nations his disciples if he really is
Lord over life and death.

This is the church's one great opportunity:
to believe in the resurrected Lord and enter his

service without reservation, to proclaim his word without abridgement and fulfill his commission without fear even if it should mean "becoming like him in his death." The church's whole existence depends on a miracle: that he who was dead has risen again and is now with them all their days. The church itself is a participation in this miracle. She would not exist if Christ's resurrection power was not at work in her. A new era dawned when Christ rose from the dead. The course of the world reached its first point of fulfillment. When Christ's lifeless and martyred corpse rose from the grave in a new form, then for the first time this fallen and perishable creation approached "the freedom of the glory of the children of God" (Rom. 8:21). This renewed reality where death is engulfed by life is, of course, the end goal for the whole course of the world. "According to his promise we are waiting for new heavens and a new earth" (2 Pet. 3:13). This all-changing rebirth where death is swallowed up by life and the perishable dresses itself in the imperishable has become the reality in the Savior's resurrection. It is in this single point where the new life is already now revealed in the perdition *hell* of the world. Yet the same power also works obscurely. It lives even now as a mystery of God in every point where the world participates in Christ's life. In the midst of this world that is now marred by evil, suffering, and destruction, the power of the resurrection is at work. Even this is hidden as a mystery just as the divinity of Christ was hidden in his human form. Yet it is here. He clothes himself in an external form that can be seen by everyone and heard by every human ear. This outer form is the Word, the sacraments, the divine service, the congregation, and the office of holy ministry. Everything that the Resurrected One does and works, all that he draws into his sphere of life, all that he justifies and sanctifies, all that he uses in some way as a means for his grace, it is permeated by the hidden power of the resurrection. And the totality of all that is the resurrection's new life in death's old world is this: the holy, catholic church.

So, the church is a mystery to the world. She stands in the midst of the world but does not belong to the world. She is at once visible and invisible. She can be depicted and described, mapped, and registered in statistical tables—and she is at the same time intangible and inconceivable to all those who are not themselves born again into the hidden life in God. When the world attempts to comprehend the church, it can never see anything but the externals. What it sees, it interprets in analogy to phenomena of this world. It conceives of her as a movement or an association—and consequently cannot understand why the church is not like other associations that can reform their statutes and suit themselves a little better according to the desires of men. Or it conceives of the church as an outlook on life, a moral system, or a philosophical interpretation of life, and cannot at all understand why the church should be so intransigent in questions about small changes concerning its doctrine or its traditional principles. That which is the church's soul, her creating spirit, her new life, it is and remains a mystery to those who stand outside— until the moment when the fire is kindled in their own hearts, and they too are incorporated into this completely newly created context that proceeds from the Resurrected One.

So, the church's task is unreasonable, just as unreasonable in our century. Every new generation needs to confess that Jesus is Christ. This means to lead every new generation to faith in the Resurrected One who won life for us when he gave himself to death. Here there is no lasting result, nothing that of itself is included in the inheritance from fathers to children. If the church does not do what is impossible for people to do—to lead souls to faith in the crucified Christ, which has been an offense and foolishness for people from the beginning—then she ceases to exist. Within the course of a single generation, she can dissolve and disappear.

So, her opponents in all times have also predicted her impending downfall. Sound reason has been certain for two thousand years that it was only a matter of time before this monstrous fantasy would be finally overcome. Had it depended on the church's own members, the opponents would have been proved right long ago. Within Christianity there has been found so much blindness and misunderstanding, so much selfishness and inability to realize one's own little piece of the love that is still the most important commandment in our law, that it more than well should have caused the dissolution of a human organization.

It is not our doing that despite everything the church has remained, but the promise that the gates of hell cannot overcome her—and that he who gave us the promise is also able to keep it.

In this constantly renewed crisis, the church must constantly hold this before her eyes. Otherwise, it lies close at hand for her to try make herself safe by appealing to this world's political or social associations. She can build up a hierarchical system that binds itself to the power brokers of the day and try to guarantee that people should at least show an external respect for the church and her orders. She can settle down as the state church and trust that the state shall pay the important wages, organize the new congregations, and guarantee the Christian foundation of the schools. It can seem safe for the church to rest in the state's arms. Yet this is a fraudulent security. Certainly, it can be both useful and important for the church to work with the state, and to a certain degree it is co-organized with society's organizations. However, the church is never secure by getting a secured economy or an external respect for her holy dealings guaranteed by the state. The church is never secure here on Earth. In every generation, she must fight the apostolic fight to lead man from darkness to light, from unbelief to faith, from death to life. She always remains in a relationship of tension with the surrounding world. She can always count on being misunderstood or hated. She lives in a world that shall be baptized, among men who Christ wants to reach with the forgiveness of sins, but who themselves react before the divine love with an emotion that tries to defend itself with cynicism, with a helpless fear that expresses itself in bullying and mockery — or sometimes with a dark and unreasonable hate.

When the church did not want to accept this, and instead attempted to get respect with the help of the law and sheriffs, she has always lost. She has experienced this peculiarity: the law is used against her most burning servants, and the sheriffs intervene against those who really understand what the Gospel means. The legally enforced appearance of Christendom has shown itself to be the bitterest enemy of the pious who take the church's message seriously.

So seen from one point of view, the church's situation is always just as critical. The Gospel will always be preached before a generation that will not receive it because of all the selfishness that is our innate nature, and that chafes at loving God and serving our neighbor. What Paul says applies to every age: "the days are evil" (Eph. 5:16). Yet concerning every age it also applies to equal degree: "Behold, now is the favorable time" (2 Cor. 6:2). The days are evil because "the spirit now at work in the sons of disobedience" (Eph. 2:2) is always just as active. He who does his best to live in the love of Christ must always count on a mysterious opposition, an irrational hate, that he would never have encountered if he had not confessed Christ. Yet at the same time, every age is to an equal degree "the favorable time." When the Gospel begins to be preached in the world a light has been lit that darkness can never overpower. Powers have been set in motion that give man completely new opportunities. There is one who has gone out to seek the perishing and lost. It is a new and peculiar kingdom that approaches us. Blessed is the invitation: "behold, now is the day of salvation" (2 Cor. 6:2).

For us Christians this means that we consider this as did Paul, who almost brutally and yet with the liberating certainty of faith set before the eyes of his contemporaries: "if Christ has not been raised, then our preach-

ing is in vain and your faith is in vain . . . and
you are still in your sins . . . but in fact Christ
has been raised from the dead, the first fruits of
those who have fallen asleep" (1 Cor. 15:14–20).

Everything depends on this: that Christ
is risen, that God's Son "was delivered
up for our trespasses and raised for our justification" (Rom. 4:25).

We should also be harshly reminded that
Christianity is an ill-tolerated stranger in the
world, so we have no reason to sit down and
complain. "Do not be surprised, brothers, that
the world hates you" (1 John 3:13). "Know that
it has hated me before it hated you" (John 15:18).
Let us praise God that the opposition is there.
It is the important opposition between the gospel of love and the wisdom of this world that
proclaims that everyone is our neighbor. It is
an inevitable conflict between the law of life
and that of death, between the message of the
Resurrected One and the dogma of everything's
transience. This world proclaims two cardinal
teachings: that the innermost driving force of

everything is selfishness and that everything living is helplessly addicted to death. Both of these propositions are subverted by the Gospel. Egoism is neither natural nor excusable. Just as little is mortality natural or inevitable. Man is created for life, to love as children of God. Every other way of living is abnormal and wrong. To live for oneself is to break with God. Therefore, Christ's Gospel is unbearable to this world. "It hates me because I testify about it that its works are evil" (John 7:7).

The opposition is also a sign that God is active. It is evidence that he has not taken his hand from us. So, there is no reason to despair — but all the more to ask after God's will and to learn from God's deeds in the past.

Within and through the history of the world passes a holy history. Within this which is seen to be meaningless jumbles there is an interwoven context that reveals God's meaning. God has intervened in history. He has operated and spoken. He has sent his messengers and his Son. He has resolved the unresolvable problem:

how the unrepentant egotistical man would be able to become children of the immutable holy God. He has carried out his saving and sanctifying work century after century and is active amongst us to this very day.

There are also events in history that preserve his meaning for all coming ages. It is God's message to all people in his spoken and written word. There have always been epochs when men experienced, interpreted, and realized the Gospel in a manner that has something to teach all coming generations.

So, the program given for the Christian church is that in her constantly critical situation she is to seek after norms and programs for her activity: this means to see what God has done. It means to learn from holy history. It means to take care of the inheritance that has been entrusted to us. The program is the same as during the time of the apostles: preserve what has been entrusted to you. Keep to what you have learned and what you have gained knowledge of. You know from whom you have learned. You know from childhood the Holy Scriptures that could give you wisdom. Let us uneasily hold fast to the confession of hope.

If today we seek to learn with complete honesty from the history that the church before us has experienced, then this is not the same as romanticism or traditionalism. A state, a folk movement, or an old generation can have its traditions. They have very relative worth. They are only expressions for what men thought at one time. They might be a shackle that has to be broken so that life can continue. It is different with the church. Christendom is always the living work of the living Lord. It is Christ who in every generation creates Christendom. So, there is always something remaining in this living church, something that is not only an expression for the way people of that time thought. In the church's greatest epochs, the eras when Christ carries out great things in his church, something always happens that is not simply dated, not simply determined by the problems of that generation and neither determined to merely answer that generation's problems. To listen to this and to learn from it is not historically romantic, but faith in the Resurrected One who is with us every day, and faith that the work he carries out today always makes use of the means he has given us in the past. This Lord who is living in all times comes to live in every age through the Word he has already spoken and the work he has already done.

———•◦•———

If a person wants to see what true Christianity means, if he wants to learn how Christ's church lives and works, if he wants to know how a man's soul is saved, then a man shall first and foremost go back to the days of the apostles, martyrs, and church fathers; next, a person should set himself down and contemplate the message of the Reformation; and finally a man should not forget the grace-filled *seelsorgers*[1]

———

1 The word "seelsorgers" comes from German and has no exact English equivalent. Its literal meaning is "one who

that God gave our church in the last century and through whom he gave the church profound awakenings from which all coming ages will have something to learn.

This is the threefold inheritance—the early church, the reformation, and the awakenings—that should now be administered and brought to life. Here this means both to preserve and share, both to learn from the past and make it living for the present. Essentially, this is two sides of the same thing. It is of course the Resurrected One and the living Lord who worked everything in the past. To keep fast to the old is to remain in him. Yet then the work is at the same time new, renewed by the Resurrected One himself. The more completely we live by the powers that have built God's church before, then all the more clearly will Christ show us the way we must now go.

So our working plan is this: to learn from the past to be able to meet tomorrow, to dive

---

cares for souls," and suggests a person whose work concerns the spiritual well-being of others, such as a pastor.

as deeply into the church's great river of life so that we are prepared to proclaim Christ's Word before new men and live his life in the manner that belongs to this new century in the church's history.

Eastern philosophy
groups
West philosophy
more focus on Jesus
individual

I.
INHERITANCE FROM THE EARLY CHURCH

HOLY SCRIPTURE

First and foremost, our church is character-ized by the fact that she survived the apostolic era. I intentionally say survived. The Lutheran Church is a branch of the Apostolic Church, a part of that church that still lives today and once listened to Peter and Paul, Ignatius and Ire-naeus. We too are late-born limbs of the church of martyrs and catacombs, the world-conquer-ing and worldwide church. Every Sunday we confess that we belong to her, the one, holy, and catholic church. During the first days of the church this was evidence of true Christendom that one "holds fast to the apostolic teaching." There have always been fanatical spirits, sectarians, and embezzlers that wanted to change the apostolic message or thought they could interpret it better and clearer than the apostles themselves.

To "hold fast to the apostolic teaching" means first and foremost to hold fast to the Holy Scriptures. It was the mother church that gave us our Bible. This, however, should not be understood as if the mother church is the source of the Word. The Word existed before. The prophetic Word had gone out. The Gospel was proclaimed. The holy history was a fact. Not everything had yet been set to writing, but everything was there as the complete work of salvation. Over this Word the church has never been lord. It has been given to her invitingly and steadfastly. However, the mother church received the great task to gather, to fix in writing, to set the holy books apart and give them as an inheritance to the church of the future.

So here the early church has given us an inheritance that is applicable for all times and all people. In this regard the work is finished. There is nothing to add or to take from the divine Word. It is inexhaustible and constantly new. Sometimes it seems silent, mysterious, and without relevance to our reality. Then suddenly a new situation arises, and the Word, that seemed to have been dead, is full of life and authority. The Word shows that it constantly has something new to say to the questions of the day, if a person only returns to it with his questions, day after day.

Nothing can be more important than that God's Word is really taken seriously as God's Word—first and foremost by the church's own servants. Nothing can so weaken a pastor's ability to help his fellow man than his own disbelief concerning the Word. It is of course the Word that creates the church, that awakens and sanctifies people, that builds up the congregation and gives faith as an inheritance to the next generation. The Word is the manner of God's presence among us. It has pleased God to take his dwelling in this Word. This is the Bible's own view of the Word, that with new emphasis has been put forward by the most recent scholarship: God is in this Word. It has gone out from his mouth. It has the power to establish and tear down. It is Spirit and Life.

Jesus continues his earthly wandering in this Word. He takes form among us through the Word. Where the Word has gone out from him, there he himself calls disciples and carries out the same work among them that he carried out during his earthly days: he awakens their faith, reveals his mystery, and lets the light fall upon mysterious contexts that man alone can never fathom.

So, to pass over the divine Word means to break with God. It means to place oneself outside the sphere of influence where God carries out his work of salvation. The apostasy from the Word not only happens in that a person quits using it. The decisive apostasy happens in that moment when a person no longer receives it as God's

Word. The insidious thing is that a person can both read and exposit the Word in such a way that essentially denies its divine character. A person can read it with an arrogance that considers himself capable of deciding what is acceptable and what ought to be eliminated. A person can receive it as a departure point for observations that only reproduces the thoughts of men that are just now popular and commonly accepted. There is a good deal in such a sermon that can say approximately the same as God's Word, and yet is not a proclamation of God's Word. The proclaimer has not gone to the Word to hear what his Lord says. He has not bowed to the Word and received it as a message that he himself in no way is lord over and which for just that reason has power over others, a Word that is not the pastor's, not the era's, not common opinions, but proceeds from the almighty God himself.

It is truly peculiar that in the last half century many debates concerning the Bible commonly seem to have arisen because every person naturally recognizes the mystery of God's Word, such that he knows how God's Word ought to be procured, and so he could decide, for example, if the Pentateuch ought to be called God's Word. In actual fact, the divine Word is a mystery before which unbelief stands just as helpless as when it stands before the person of Christ, before the divine essence, or before God himself. A person can encounter Jesus without understanding that he has seen the Father. The church can be both seen and described without discovering anything other than an all-too-human institution. A person can perceive God in the conscience or see him in nature without learning to know the living God. In the same way a person can both read and analyze the Bible without either perceiving or understanding that it is God who speaks there.

God really does not belong to the world that a person has at his disposal. He cannot learn to know him independently of how he stands before him. God steps into our world,

God is jealous for us.

into history, into our thoughts and hearts. Yet in the same moment that he is there, there is also the divine demand for love and obedience. God is a consuming fire, a holy love that gives everything and demands everything. It is impossible to stand as an objective observer before God. With the right of a creator, he makes claim on his own, and with a father's right he seeks our reciprocal love. A man can either give God his due and this love — or deny it to him. An encounter with God always means taking a position. It is always bound with faith or denial, with childlike love or slavish fear and dismissiveness that can take all sorts of forms from complacency to blasphemy.

Such as God is, so now also is his Word. It is a Word with power and authority that places a man in a situation where he must bow in repentance and faith or try to push away from his Father and Creator. The authority of this Word is not an external, confirmable fact that a man can calmly and objectively test and weigh. It is God's own authority. Here God himself speaks to his human children. He speaks in wrath and grace, in holiness and love. He rebukes our sins, describes our helplessness and our powerless conceit, our attempts to play as if we were grown when we are in fact children, our cruelty, and our fear of death. He also speaks about his own fatherly heart's longing for his children, about his efforts that span the millennia to open our eyes and make it possible for us to receive the great work of salvation in Jesus Christ, the great mystery that says: Christ died for our sins, Christ rose from the dead and blesses us, Christ lives in our hearts through faith.

This is the message of salvation that is God's Word to us. It is these things that it pleases him to reveal to us through the Scriptures. The Gospel is "the power of God for salvation . . . revealing righteousness from God" (Rom. 1:16–17). Here God himself is present, here God's hand is outstretched and touches our hearts. Here, he who has ears to hear encounters his Father and his Redeemer.

Here, there is an infinite difference between the Bible and every other book. It is this mystery of God's Word that the profane [*secular*] reason can never fathom. That the Bible is God's Word means the same thing to profane reason as that it is an inerrant source for history and for scientific knowledge. So, the old Adam does not interest himself with God's message of salvation. He turns the means of grace that is God's Word into a reference work. He turns the admonition to repentance into a history of the world. He should receive salvation from these Scriptures. Instead, he gathers geological notes or prophecies concerning the latest political developments in the world.

It is this fundamentally profane view that distracted so many of the debates about the Bible at the turn of the century. The thought is that if the Bible is God's Word, then it must be able to be show this through a scientific analysis of its royal genealogies, its chronologies, or its zoological and ethnographic notations men believe they have found in it. So, the debate descended into unfruitful quarreling about ruminating hares or about Jonah's sea voyage. Even when a person discussed the Epic of Gilgamesh or Sennacherib's siege of Jerusalem in a more scientific manner, it often happened from the obvious assumption that God's Word could be examined like a doctoral thesis, and that the matter of its divine authority could be set aside at any licentiate seminar.

unprincipled

It is this naïve, thoroughly profane view of the Bible that must give way for a deeper and truer Christianity. We must humble ourselves and recognize the simple truth that God has the right to speak to us how he wants and that he can talk to us both with power and authority, without giving us the right to demand to receive from his Word some form of an authorized reference work to use in every scientific discipline. It has pleased God to give us the Scriptures just as they are. He has chosen precisely this form to speak to us. To everyone who wants to listen he speaks authoritatively and clearly concerning the origin of life, the purpose and meaning of this world's history, concerning man's situation, concerning the reality of sin, about his holy law, and concerning salvation through faith in Jesus — without thereby giving us a scientific description of the world that makes our human research superfluous.

How different would the Bible look if it were to be congruent with the scientific worldview of every era? Every worldview is doomed to be overcome and replaced by a new worldview. Of science's latest results there is only an unpretentious fraction that is still recognized as true after two generations. The divine truth is eternal and unchangeable. It does not lie on the same plane as the results of our own scientific research. So, God has left it to our human reason to investigate the things that we are able to research. As far as it goes, we may try to piece together bits of science's great puzzle and build out our knowledge of nature or history. However, our knowledge about God is not a product of our research efforts or our thinking. It is a fruit of God's revelation in history. It is given to us by God himself and preserves its application for all eras.

As is well known, the church has never firmly fixed any teaching about Scripture's inspiration. It only maintains what the Bible itself teaches: the prophetic Word has not come about through the will of man. It is certainly men who have spoken, but they have been driven by the Holy Spirit and spoken that which was given to them by God. So, the Bible is "inspired by God." The expression that is taken from the Bible itself means essentially "permeated by God's Spirit" or "breathed out by God" (2 Tim. 3:16). It is for this reason that this Scripture can be "profitable for teaching, for reproof, for correction, and for training in righteousness" (2 Tim. 3:16). So this Word does not merely contain teachings about God. It is itself a means of salvation. The core of the early church's belief concerning the Word could be expressed: the Word is not a teaching about God, it is a part of

God himself. The Scriptures are themselves permeated by the divine reality that they speak of.

So, the Scriptures are God's address to us
men. Perhaps a man comprehends this easier
when God speaks through his prophets, or
when the Word comes directly from the lips of
Jesus. Yet, it is the two-thousand-year experience of the church that God also speaks through
the remaining parts of Scripture, through the
historical parts, through the apostolic letters,
through the hymns of praise in the Psalter and
through the lamentations of Job. God has something to say throughout it all. Throughout it all
there are parts of the message of salvation in
Christ. If you add it all together, then a man
possesses all the knowledge of God and his
salvation that is possible to possess in this life.
A man does not gain this knowledge through
a mechanical study, no matter how unconditionally he believes in every individual statement. Still less does anyone gain it through a
subtraction process where a person believes
he could peel away the "time stamped" and

"sub-evangelical" and preserve the valuable and remaining. The mystery is found in the proper way of reading, and in the humility that wants to receive God's message.

So, it has never been easy to read the Bible. The difficulties were just as great for a cultured Roman in the fourth century as they are for a modern Western man today. It is very insightful to hear what Augustine says about his first encounter with Scripture. He found it to be worth comparing to Cicero. He did not want to bow his neck, not even a little. So, neither could his view penetrate into Scripture's spirit. Only later did he discover the mystery of the Bible: *incessu humilem, successu excelsam*, insignificant at the first encounter, but esteemed more highly with successive encounters.

We have no reason to go beyond the Bible's own doctrine of inspiration. We may not bind consciences where God himself has not bound them. Research and scholarship shall have their freedom. The historical questions that the Bible can give rise to may be debated freely. Luther, who was filled to the brim of his heart by the authority of the Word and who lived in and by its power, could speak very freely and be unbothered about such things. He knew that he did not thereby disturb God's message a hair. He listened to Scripture with a pulsating heart in order to comprehend, believe, and obey what God wanted to say. This is the great and inexhaustible truth. Here God speaks. It has pleased God to take residence in this Word and to talk to us through this book, just as it is. It is not our task to criticize, to select or change. Our task is to listen, to seek, to dig into the Word and understand it in the whole of its context in order to allow us to be fulfilled by the divine truth and be enveloped by it.

So faith in the Word does not mean the disallowance of factual biblical research. It is precisely this classical faith in the Bible as God's message that entails an unavoidable obligation for a man to thoroughly study the biblical text himself, and to pry deeper into the biblical world with all the means of science. First and foremost, this means determining the meaning that a statement had in the historical situation where it first appeared. Yet the task is not thereby completed. A biblical word often has a deeper meaning than what is immediately conceivable at the beginning. The whole Old Testament points forward to Christ. God, who allowed this big book to be such as it became, has woven this picture of Christ, who would come in the fullness of time, throughout the Scriptures. It was this that Christ taught the two disciples to understand on the road to Emmaus, when he "interpreted to them in all the Scriptures the things concerning himself" (Luke 24:27). It was this that early Christianity constantly rediscovered when they broadened their understanding of the Old Testament. The meaning of Scripture had been hidden by a veil before, but now it has been taken away, and the Word's deepest meaning stepped forward. Ever since then, that Scripture interprets Scripture has applied as a rule for all biblical exposition. The Bible is an organic unity. It possesses a final context where the different parts give sculptural relief to the one truth about Christ. Therefore, biblical theology does not stop with a historical analysis of individual expressions but strives to put forward the foundational biblical concepts in the whole of their context, so as God in fact let them live and work in the church. As Bishop Anders Nygren says: "The word of Scripture is not merely given to the people to whom it was first spoken. Its meaning does not exhaust itself in what the prophet and his contemporaries could comprehend. They did not yet live in the time of fulfillment. It was not God's purpose that everything would be laid bare and revealed before their eyes. But now Scripture is also given to us who live in the fullness of time."

Our fathers have found a series of pregnant formulations for this view of the Bible that claims its divine authority without thereby allowing a profane abuse of it. Clearly and profoundly, it comes to expression already in the energetic assertion that the Word is always law or gospel. The Word also always contains a message or a promise from God. So, it always addresses oneself. Consequently, the old fathers also said that the Word should always be read in view of salvation, so in such a way that I seek God's answer to my heart's question to God, and the way to him. For this same reason they called the Scriptures a means of grace. Where the Word is proclaimed, there God himself seeks the souls of men, there God's own Spirit is active to give us a share in the means of grace. And finally: this Holy Scripture has a center, something that is its "nucleus and star." All that God has spoken serves to reveal salvation in Jesus Christ. All that the Bible has to say about the course of the world and history has only one background and one explanation in the Gospel. The history of the world is painted in great strokes from creation to the final judgment. The picture is often stylized, the details disappear in the shadows, but the divine purpose is completely clear for those who want to see it: Our world originates from God's hand, through the rebellion of evil it has hurled it into suffering and misery; over the centuries God has prepared his salvation by fostering in Israel knowledge of the law and the hope of the Messiah; in the fullness of time he has sent his Son; and in this current era the Gospel of the forgiveness of sins is to be proclaimed to all people, so that this evil in its last great dash gathers up all of its power and is defeated for all time by the returning Lord. All this is said so that everyone should know what God has done, and so learn to know the name which is above all names: Jesus, the Lord.

So now we have touched upon one of the sorest points in the evangelical church's sick body. There is no doubt that the distress that we suffer through has one of its deepest causes in the inner weakness of the proclamation, a weakness that often bottoms out in the proclaimer's own insecurity before the Word. Every priest who has done his studies in the last quarter century recognizes this insecurity. The radical biblical criticism had set in place a violent offense to faith in the inerrancy of Scripture. Many sought resolution in a historical view of the Bible that read Scripture through the glass lens of that period, for example, and interpreted it according to the evolutionary scheme. The Bible bore witness to how Israel gradually fought itself from faith in a primitive desert god to a purified monotheism whose crown was the proclamation of Jesus concerning the loving Father. So, it was left to the Israelite folk religion to find out what had lasting value.

For many, a new day gradually dawned. Reality has a beneficial ability to correct these theories. It does not do to relativize at sickbeds. A word from God is needed, a word without reservation and reinterpretations, proceeding from the lips of the Almighty and in this moment given to precisely this anxious soul. Here the Word suddenly springs into action. It shows itself to have power. It accomplishes what human well-wishing could never be able to do. It forgives sins, it gives peace it carries through death.

Why then should it not be similar from the pulpit? Perhaps one day the pastor could let all his human concerns go and say in his heart: "At your word, Lord. . ." Then there is a new ring in his preaching, calm and steady: "So says the Lord. So speaks God. This is our savior's word to us today."

It shows itself in that preaching becomes proclamation. When the priest wants nothing else but to honestly and clearly say what God has said in his Word, when he lays the Bible before him in the pulpit, places the questions and lets the Word answer, then people begin to say: "This here is given. We receive so much in the church. . ." Perhaps (to the great shame of the pastor), a person even says: "We have never heard this before."

It is now as it was in the first century: faith comes from preaching. Yet preaching must then be delivered "in the power of Christ's Word." A preacher can be however spiritual and eloquent as he likes, he can speak both pathetically and wisely, and it still will not be a proclamation until he himself is captivated by God's Word and wants nothing other than to let the Word itself come to speak.

So, the pastor's first duty is to preach the biblical message as pure and clearly as has he can, without abbreviation and without reservation. He is God's steward, who has received in his hand the mysterious power of life and death. What God expects of his stewards is that he is found to be faithful.

So, the pastor is not a prophet. He does not go and wait for a revelation and a word from the Lord; that shall be given to him in his heart. When he does not know what he should say, he should not just pray uneasily for a moment of inspiration. He should sit down and read his Bible, look up parallel passages, make excerpts, and gather material. He should take from the old proclaimers who knew their Bibles and see what they said about the same text and what biblical truths they exposited in the context. The pastor is not a prophet. He teaches, he is placed to proclaim the old message "just as he has learned it."

Neither is the pastor a poet. He does not wait for inspiration. He does not step forward to say something that has never before been heard, or that has never before been said in such a manner. He does not set his sermon preparation on the boardwalk at the beach or the lilac arbor. He is a servant of the Word. His workplace is the study where he works with his concordance, his Greek testament, and all the other means of help he has in his library.

Least of all is the pastor a columnist. He is not there to tell little anecdotes from the tramcar or nursery or make spiritual commentary on the day's chronicles. His most eager efforts are not to get people to come, but to have something to say to them, not to be original but to be true, not to captivate but to help.

This is not to say that a pastor who wants to be a true proclaimer of the Word cannot learn anything from both prophets and poets.

The prophetic task appears very obviously in a true sermon. It is firm and spirit-filled: thus says the Lord. The pastor is not himself a prophet, but he carries the prophetic message, the revealed Word, in which God is still present and still speaks. It is this that makes a sermon come alive. It is a fundamental error if the proclamation becomes a lecture about Christian things or simply commentary on the text. The pastor is not supposed to speak about God or about contemporary matters. He is to let God speak to the contemporary. To receive this prophetic seriousness in the proclamation, the pastor must first and foremost listen to the Word himself to hear God speak to his own heart. Then it can also be useful that he sometimes keeps the Bible at hand in the pulpit and cites directly from Scripture, so that everyone can see how the answer to the soul's questions come directly from God's lips.

The poetic task in a sermon is less than essential. It is almost completely lacking in many good proclaimers. Among others it is a useful means of help that when rightly used can be a blessing. Not so that the artistic inspiration can ever give the priest any part of the message he is to present. Yet, when it comes to seeing what the message means and helps make conceivable for others, then it can be a help to possess a sense and imagination and some artistic ability. A man does not grasp the Gospel from nature. And yet it is an access point to have wide eyes for the beauty of nature. The pastor who has an eye for color and lines of play in the landscape of his homeland, he can best explain what it means that "the heavens proclaim the glory of God" or that God's "invisible being, his eternal power and divine glory can be understood through his work." In the same manner it is an access point to see the lives of men with open eyes, and everywhere read a living commentary on it, as Scripture says about the children of men. Such small observations give proclamation living details that expound the Word without solicitation in a manner that is faithful to reality so contemporary people can connect it to their reality. The powerful descriptions of death's approach in the twelfth chapter of Ecclesiastes give us an example of how the Word itself is saturated with reality and a manner of speaking that burns the Word into the memory of the hearers.

It does not hurt for the proclaimer to review his concept of preaching every now and then and attempt to eradicate the common clichés. It is always unfruitful to speak of "sin" in a general way. It only becomes an empty word to people, or binds itself to certain coarse vices which do not burden them. It is far better to try name a couple concrete sins that the context gives rise to. So Scripture itself does when it speaks of enmity, quarreling, discord, and cliquishness. Better than constantly using the words "contempt for mercy" is to seek a new picture that says what it means: the dusty confirmation Bible, hammer blows during the call to gather, radio church that is only a pretext for kitchen work. "Lovelessness" is for most people a completely empty word that does not disturb anyone. It is better to speak of grumpy answers, sulky silence, the habit of not seeing if the wife or neighbor needs a hand, the schadenfreude over another's mistakes,or another of the thousands upon thousands of expressions that sinful nature daily embraces. If the pastor has any similarity with a columnist, it should be in just this quick, sure comprehension of such details. However, here is demanded more than an ability to observe. Here we need the Spirit's work that daily exposes our own old Adam—and thereby gives us an inexhaustible storehouse of examples for the depravity of sin—and teaches us to see all the congregational member's faults and weaknesses with a *seelsorger's* warmhearted concern.

It takes a lot of work to get away from the common clichés. Yet it is well-used courage. Next to the necessary work of mining God's Word and basing the whole sermon on God's Word, there is nothing so urgent as to try find precisely the small details of reality that give God's Word the right application to the people, for whom one is placed to preach.

Nohrborg, Schartau, and the other classics in our church are untouched masters, both when it comes to biblical anchoring and the sharp application to us men. A man can never spend too much time learning from them when it comes to learning what a sermon should contain. When it comes to language and form, a person should not copy them. In stylistics they are not role models. Their prose suffers badly from the common faults of their era: dependent on Latin ideals of style and German prosody. There is nothing biblical in dressing God's Word up in sentence structures that are foreign to us. On the contrary, faithfulness to the Word demands that we seek to speak just as folksily, clearly, and powerfully as the Word itself speaks. That which distinguishes the Word is first and foremost that it is a message, something that is spoken directly to us people. So it is in conflict with the spirit of the Bible to speak in generalities and abstractions, to speak about something without at the same time speaking to someone. Even when a person speaks in the third person, the proclamation may never lose its character of being an urgent message that concerns precisely those who now sit in the church listening. The proclamation shall therefore make every possible effort to speak clearly

and understandably. The weight of the content
has nothing to do with the weight in the form.
The heavy form is solely a hindrance that both
can and ought to be done away with. From the
old masters, we could learn the essentials, the
biblical contents, the ready outline, the pregnant expressions. Then we have both freedom
and duty to speak so that the message can be
received by just these men who listen to us on
this day.

awakening = Law/Gospel sinner + need a savior

work of the people *means*

LITURGY AND SPIRITUAL AWAKENING

awakening = open

The Word creates the church. Already in the
earliest days of the church, the Word gave congregational life the forms that have since followed us through the millennia. This applies
to both the forms that look to be improvised
and erratic, and those that seem unchangeably
fixed. This applies both to the side of the church
life that we call awakening, and to that which
is called liturgy. Both are creations of the Word,

awakening is understanding who we are

liturgy 2000 yrs.

and both belong to that inheritance that we are
called to preserve.

Both liturgy and awakening are found in
the Apostolic Church. They were already spoken of at the first Pentecost. "Now when they
heard this they were cut to the heart and said
to Peter and the rest of the apostles, 'Brothers,
what shall we do?'" (Acts 2:37) This is awakening. "And day by day they were attending the
temple together . . . and Peter and Paul went up
to the temple at the hour of prayer, the ninth
hour" (Acts 2:42; 3:1). This is liturgy.

Both have followed the church throughout the whole of her history. Admittedly, their
manners look very dissimilar. Awakening is
like the flickering flames above a bed of coals.
It glimmers, spreads, rises to the sky, and
seems to be gone again. Its connection with
the early church seems to be broken by dark
intervals. And yet the connection is there, for
the Spirit is one and the same. He who cut
hearts on the day of Pentecost, and the Word
that kindles the mysterious flame, is the same

powerful Word that once passed over the lips of the apostles.

The liturgy's connection with the apostolic age is clearer. It has flown through the ages as an unbroken stream. Its primary spring was already there in the synagogue. It is not only individual words which it has unceasingly used such as amen, hallelujah, hosanna, but the whole structure of our Sunday communion service (High Mass) clearly shows its kinship to this worship service (Divine Service) that Jesus himself celebrated as a boy in the synagogue at Nazareth, and in which he appeared as an adult when he stepped forward to expound upon the Scriptures. To the old divine service of the synagogue the apostolic church included the new creation that she received from the Savior himself and which is the heart of all the liturgy: Holy Communion. Just as it is celebrated even today with alternating chants, the preface, and the Sanctus, in all this it is essentially a work of the first century.

The unbroken connection with the apostolic era is also revealed in the external forms of the liturgy. The altar is the one place in modern society where a person can still (with unbroken tradition!) use the clothing that was used by the people of antiquity. Under the vaulted ceiling of the church, a person can still hear the tones that preserved some of the ring in the Psalms that the Master and his disciples sang after eating the paschal lamb. The sanctuary is the one place in our land where a person can still hear the best of the medieval tonal art, or even see the great treasures of art from that era as a living ingredient of our culture. There is nothing in modern Western society that holds nearly as much ancient culture or so many venerable traditions as our Divine Service.[1]

---

1 Here I chose Divine Service to translate "High Mass" (högmässa), though normally the word gudstjänst is the word behind divine service, which is the literal translation of gudstjänst. Often gudstjänst, which corresponds to the German word Gottesdienst, is also translated as divine service or sometimes simply as worship, depending on context. English-speaking Lutherans use the word Divine Service in the same way that High Mass is used here. If Divine Service is capitalized it is translating High Mass and is meant to indicate the Sunday worship service with Holy Communion.

Of course, this is not essential. The deepest meaning of the liturgy is found in that it is a form that the Spirit himself created to preserve and deepen that life which the same Holy Spirit awakens in his church.

Awakening is the fire's flame that flares up in the dead soul. The fire burns in the breast, the sinner feels the sting in the conscience. In a time of worry and anxiousness he asks: what shall I do? And the Spirit answers by revealing the seriousness of sin and the boundless mercy of Christ.

The liturgy is the same Spirit's work to preserve the flame that has been kindled. It is a means to incorporate the awakened into the church's communion. It is a form for walking in the light, a path that leads through the years where the soul is constantly called again to unite with the royal priesthood that does its temple service before God's altar with prayers and songs of praise, receives the Lord's Supper, and calmly listens to the Lord's Word.

Liturgy and awakening have often come to stand in opposition to each other. It was not so in the earliest church and ought not to be so today either. They are the work of the same Spirit, parts of the same inheritance. They both have the right to be there, and they both have the right to form themselves according to their own idiosyncrasies too.

Spiritual awakening and liturgy partially speak different languages, and so they must. The instrument of awakening is the spoken Word, a Word with prophetic authority, powerful enough to crush the heart's hard stone and at the same time appeal with the Gospel's complete sincerity. The language of awakening is often related to the everyday. God seeks the perishing and the lost. The Word grasps after he who is not at home in God's courts and is perhaps not trained to understand the biblical concepts. So, the language of awakening does not speak of Jesse's root, or the key of David. It speaks to children of the age in the language of the things that they have forgotten but need to hear.

It is completely different with the liturgy. Its instrument is also the Word, but as it pours out from the deepest springs. The liturgy "imparts wisdom among the mature" (1 Cor. 6:2). It makes use of all the wealth of Scripture, all the content-saturated symbols and the hidden foreshadowing of Christ in the Old Testament. It takes from the prayers in the Psalter and prays them anew. It listens to the prophets and dives into the Gospel's deepest mysteries. It loves precisely that which only slowly reveals itself and which constantly gives the mind something new to contemplate. For just that reason the liturgy constantly turns back to the same holy forms; it even dares to use the hidden wisdom of Scripture. So it also loves a music that contains inexhaustible depth of humble worship and expectant joy behind its apparent simplicity. It loves to lift hearts to God with the kyrie's guarded tones or the preface's dignified joy. In all this it is very different from awakening.

A person could perhaps express the difference by comparing awakening to the Lord's fire that fell upon Elijah's water-drenched altar. It is the erratic intervention of the sovereign

God that reveals his power among the heathen. Again, the liturgy is the fire that burns on the altar in the temple and that Scripture mandates shall never be extinguished. Awakening is prophetic, the liturgy is pastoral. Awakening is like lightning from above that kindles new fire. The liturgy is the Lord's flame that burns among us and gives light as it warms the faithful.

Now this means that we give both awakening and liturgy their rightful, early Christian places in congregational life. We always need awakening, not only because the church must always be a missionary church reaching out to those who stand outside, but also because the church's most faithful members also always need awakening. Every old Adam is similarly inclined to doze off, to turn the Christian life into a dead routine, to use the forms of the liturgy as a means to cocoon oneself in complacency and unrepentance. It is not hard to get in order a religious way of life that suits one's own self and allows the old Adam to make himself lord again. A person can periodically go to church and commune. A person can enjoy the beautiful church music and the stately sanctuaries. A person can be honestly convinced of the orthodox doctrine and love true proclamation. At the same time a man can be steeped in a self-love, pleased with himself, pleased with his pious accomplishments and indifferent to the worries and burdens of other men who are before his own eyes every day. The Holy Spirit always needs to awaken slumbering souls, stir up the dust, send the old Adam packing, and breathe new life into dead bones. Awakening is never superfluous when we remain in the flesh.

Just as necessary is the liturgy. There can be no normal congregational life without the liturgy. The sacraments need a form. Of course, worship (divine service) must be performed in a certain manner. For short periods it can do to live on improvision and forms that constantly change and are newly created. A person can pray purely free prayers and create a new ritual for every worship occasion. However, the possibilities exhaust themselves quickly. A person

must then repeat himself, and then the process
of building rituals comes into full swing. In circles that attempt to live without any forms, a
new form is always being made. A person may
regularly return to beloved songs, particular
prayers are constantly repeated, there are firmly
fixed yearly traditions with certain traditional
ceremonies. And it is hardly uncharitable to
say that the new forms that come about in this
manner are more homely and profane than the
old liturgy. They contain less of God's Word,
they typically do not pray and speak with Scripture's locution, they are not keen to grab from
the whole of Scripture's contents but are content with one or another that seems particularly
striking or popular. The new liturgy that grows
in this way is poorer, less biblical, and less nour-
ishing for the soul than the old liturgy a person
had before.

So, both awakening and liturgy have their
given place in the church. This does not stop
the liturgy from appearing as the enemy of
awakening, just as awakening can be made the

opponent of liturgy. Here there is a tension that has made itself embarrassingly obvious even within our own Lutheran history.

Awakening can in fact appear as the liturgy's most dangerous enemy. The liturgy also has many other enemies, first and foremost the apathetic passiveness that will enjoy or listen to a divine service instead of participating in it. A fully occupied church is not the same thing as a congregation. Where hands no longer fold, where heads no longer bow in prayer and there are no longer voices — they can be striving or noisemaking — joining in the hymns there is no longer a real divine service. The liturgy is always active. Lazy, dead passivity is always its enemy.

Yet awakening can be an even more dangerous enemy. At least worldly cares usually know that they are not more spiritual than the liturgy. However, the liturgically opposed awakening passes itself off as just that worship in spirit and truth that the Father wants to have. It condemns and despises liturgy. Though, sometimes it can be a legitimate critique in the spirit of the prophets. If the pastor plays with his nails during the offertory and searches for the general prayer of the church in the hymnal while he kneels at the altar after preaching, then it is quite proper to speak about dead deeds for which a man must repent if he is to return to a true ministry before the one, true God. Yet it is therefore not said that this ministry must consist in laying aside the vestments and ceasing to sing the preface in favor of free prayers and setting up house churches and singing the latest melodies from the dance halls. In the same way there are occasions when it is right to cite the Lord's wrath in the words of the prophet Amos: "Take away from me the noise of your songs, / to the melody of your harps I will not listen" (Amos 5:23). For example, when the cantor has his newspaper on the organ lectern, or the choir members disappear before the sermon, or the church council departs immediately after a magnificent Advent vespers service for the mayor's home to booze it up. There is dead liturgy, or perhaps it is better to say dead hearts who let all the treasures of the liturgy pass by, or who understand being present but cleverly avoid everything that might lead to conversion. There is also a faulty way to use a rich and beautiful liturgy that makes it sluggish, artificial, stamped with complacency or desire to make one's own person shine. The problem is not the liturgy. Nor can the problem be remedied by abandoning God's good Word that a person ought to take to heart. It is certainly true that it is better to sing dance hall melodies with the heart turned to Jesus than pious chorales while thinking of dinner or the last congregational quarrel. Yet it is thereby not true that the dance hall melodies in and of themselves are better suited to express a pious disposition than a good old church chorale.

So, awakening goes wrong when it condemns the liturgy. There is often a good deal of self-righteousness and self-love in the condemnation. The old Adam is an unsurpassed economic politician. He always lands on his feet. If a man is seriously awakened, it does not take long before his old Adam tries to use the new situation. Naturally, it may be done with pious deeds and under constant assertion that it happens to God's glory. Even under such assertions the old man reestablishes his governance. The deeds of the flesh begin again, not in the form of "looseness, drunkenness, and wild living" — then it would immediately be recognized — but perhaps as "stubbornness, discord, and cliquishness." The reasoning is quite simple: because he himself has been awakened one way or another, then this way has to be the correct one. "The only true way" as the old Adam adds quite imperceptibly. Because at the time of his awakening the Gospel was not read, no collected or written prayer prayed, and no one sang "All Glory Be To God On High," then such things cannot be means for salvation. Perhaps the old Adam adds: "Moreover, it feels much warmer and more beautiful in the heart when a person can pray for himself or give his own testimony or sing the new songs." Presumably, the old Adam does not say that out loud. He only notes that he thrives and feels comfortable in these new clothes as well. If a person could only hear his own voice, speak a little about himself, be part of the decision, be caressed by beautiful melodies that could fit well in any operetta, then a person could tolerate being called a Christian. For spice in everything a person can happily break the rod over the liturgists and pastors in the congregation and the narrow-minded slaves of the law who maintain that a person ought to participate regularly in the Divine Service.

Now this is the coarsest form. At its side there is another sort of averseness to the liturgy, one that is humanly understandable even if it is not legitimate. There are many people who find it hard to find their way in the liturgical forms. All liturgy demands an overcoming of the self. The individual has to become part of a praying congregation. A person must immerse himself so far into communion with others that he can pray the same words as them, follow the liturgy's rhythm of confession of sin and praise, feel the same joy and the same repentance as the others. Every Christian should do this. He is a member of Christ's body. He does not live to please himself, but as part of an organism. He who will not subordinate himself in such a communion is no Christian, for a man cannot be a Christian by himself. He who does not love his brother that he has seen in the church pew and at the altar for communion, not even so much that he can pray and sing, rejoice and tremble with him, he shall not imagine that he can love the God who he has not seen, or that he can worship him in spirit and truth at home in his closet. Yet it is noticeable that there are forms for devotion that feel natural for some people so that they almost immediately find their way in them, while other people have an infinitely hard time getting anything out of them. So, the church must be heartfelt and rich. She must be able to give her children what they best need and can best receive, assuming that she really gives them God's word and communion with him. Obviously, she must have a form for everyone's common worship, a place where all can be gathered. This place is the Divine Service. Here a man has the right to demand that everyone be present. Everyone should orient himself so that he enters this communion as a praying and serving member who does not only demand to receive something, but first and foremost comes to give his contribution to the common devotion. If in the name of awakening a person puts himself at odds with the Divine Service, then he abuses the Christian communion. This is often done in the name of freedom. This freedom that a person demands in turn means bondage to the great many. It means that a person allows certain special interests to characterize that which should be the common possession of all. A person wants to press his right to worship according to his own head. If he does not get to do this, he does not thrive with the others and perhaps breaks up communion. It is here that we find what is unchristian about it all, and it is here that every ecclesiastical movement must test itself. If awakening will not even

live with the liturgy that is found in the Divine
Service, then it has its place outside the church's
communion and can no longer be counted as a
living movement within the church.

Aside from the Divine Service there must
be freedom. A person cannot rectify all the
church's worship and edification. There must
be found full freedom for devotional forms that
really serve to edify; there may then be preaching on the weekdays, catechetical instruction
at home, canonical hours, or other such things.
A person shall only demand — of himself and
others — that the forms of worship that a person
experiments with for the best do not happen
at the expense of the great communion in the
Divine Service.

If liturgy can sometimes accuse awakening
of misunderstanding, so can awakening have
reason to say that it is often not respected, or
perhaps not even tolerated, on behalf of some
friends of liturgy. There is therefore reason to
also say a word about liturgy being the worst
enemy of awakening.

Awakening also has a series of enemies, but hardly any of them can be so dangerous as a false liturgy. Namely, if the liturgy wants to be bad it can be an almost impenetrable armor for the old Adam. What shall the Holy Spirit do with a man who goes to communion more regularly than anyone else in the congregation, who prays for three-quarters or a whole hour every day, and who prays good, lovely prayers out of the Psalms, or the classic Lutheran prayer books, who reads his daily considerations or his compline every evening and devotes himself to silent meditation after every reception of the Lord's Supper, but because of all this only becomes more and more convinced of being somewhat a better man who gathers a noteworthy capital before the all-seeing God, and who perhaps during all of this neglects his earthly duties, his studies, his administrative tasks or the fostering of his children, to speak well of those who think differently and does not love anyone but himself and his holy rites? Every visit of the Holy Spirit is normally wasted on such a man so long as he moves within his habitual circles. He must come like a windstorm upon him, tear apart all his pious displays, and show him that he is a proud, conceited, self-absorbed and merciless sinner who does not deserve better than to be eternally cast from the face of God. To carry out this work the Holy Spirit can sometimes use a book, or a human destiny that ruthlessly exposes the pious game. Sometimes he uses life's conditions and puts the homemade saint in a dangerous situation where there is nothing left to glorify him. Still his usual means are the preached word, the prophetic message with the spirit of awakening. Nor is it extraordinarily characteristic of the false liturgy that it does not like the prophetic word that flashes down like lightning and does not respect any pious game rules. The false liturgy would rather clip the wings of the Word. It gladly has the sermon as part of the liturgy, framed by liturgical formulas and hymn verses, presented with disciplined caution in a language that has allowed concrete and offensive actuality to fall away.

Neat and tidy, it brings forth the old truths but never truly mentions a single one of the daily struggles where the old man raises his head and can be caught. This false liturgy can enter into a particular unification with those who were once awakened. It can accept the old preaching language and the time-honored word. But they have lost their edge, they lie so far away from everyday sins that the unrepentant heart can listen to them with great satisfaction. Yet if one day there comes within the ceremonially progressive worship a word with the old power of awakening, searching closely and healthily revealing, or if outside the divine service a man is encountered by a question or a personal word that shows how the matter of salvation can burn in a soul — then the dead churchliness becomes extremely irate and has a hundred well-considered objections to follow along.

Liturgy without awakening is possibly the most dangerous of ecclesiastical programs. It is possible to beautify the church service, to get costumes and a church choir, to order

well-attended vesper services and even to get
a certain increase in communion attendance
numbers without a single person ever really
asking: how shall a sinner be saved? Yet we all
by nature are convinced Pharisees and all just
as obviously sure that we are able to be saved
through our works, so a liturgical renewal
without a corresponding awakening of the conscience is nothing other than a certain number
of men beginning to accomplish a certain number of pious exercises in the conviction that they
now make adequate payments to the heavenly
bank account. With such a renewal the devil
himself can feel at peace. It is certainly always
questionable from his point of view when men
begin to seek out the Lord's Supper or come
within hearing distance of God's Word. Yet so
long as it is not preached in a way that can disturb a sleeping sinner, and so long as the system
only creates contented-works Christians, so long
can Satan be officially a church Christian. The
system certainly has its risks for him. A person
never knows when a little word from the epistle

reading, or a line from a hymn verse will fall on good earth. Therefore, the Prince of Darkness is never really pleased with any form of church-liness or ritualism. He would very much rather support the sort of spirituality that says that it is merely worthless custom and dead routine to go to church and attend the Lord's Supper.

Awakening needs the liturgy. An awakening that will last must foster a devotional life that keeps from wearing out over the long haul, and which can become an inheritance for children and grandchildren. A sound awakening shall therefore be focused on leading men to the divine service and communion, to teach them to celebrate the divine service in a right way and to understand, to become familiar with churchly books. It is an inflexible demand that already during confirmation a person needs to teach them to understand altar service and to navigate the hymnal, just as they can barely sing the liturgical melodies that are used in the church of their home congregation. Just as we preach over the chief parts of the catechism, we could gladly preach at times about the chief parts of the divine service, over the threefold holy, and over such words of Scripture as "Lord, have mercy," "Glory be to God on high," "The Lord be with you," and "Behold the Lamb of God who takes away the sin of the world."

Awakening can also serve the liturgy. Where men are awakened there is new life in the old forms of devotion. There is new seriousness in the confession of sin and new joy and power in the hymns of praise. Old, beautiful customs become more than tradition. They become an expression of newborn life, the same life that once created the custom and that now fills it with new sincerity and warmth.

Awakening shall one day cease. It belongs to this world, where men still sleep the sleep of sin. When Christ wakes them on the last great day, then there will no longer be any need for awakening. Then it comes to be just as forgotten and unthinkable as the hospital and child welfare boards. However, the liturgy shall remain. What Scripture also uses to give expression to the ineffable which then begins, it gives us with pictures of a heavenly liturgy, a holy service before the throne of God, with songs of praise, powerful as the noise of great waters with golden bowls full of smoke and with innumerable crowds who fall down and worship before him who is King of kings and the Lord of lords.

The liturgy in the church is a beginning to the eternal song of praise, an earthly expression for the contents of eternity, and the foundational tone of all of existence: thanksgiving never stops before the Creator and Father of everything. Already in this earthly poverty the liturgy contains something of the heavenly beauty, the blessed perception of the ineffable presence and the great joy to be able to sacrifice everything to be one with Christ.

DOGMA

While we are now talking about the inheritance from the early church, it has gone as it usually always goes, and we have become caught up in the questions that are burning for today's situation. This is because the inheritance does not concern dead goods. If one possesses the inheritance, then it works. A person cannot speak about the Word or the liturgy without beginning to speak about conversion and new life. The same applies to dogma, the sacraments, the office, and everything else we inherited from the early church.

A generation ago early church dogma was often regarded with a half-compassionate superiority. In some places they still do so—if a person is really a generation after his time. Scholars have come to a completely different assessment. No one who knows what the matter entails would now be able to sound the old battle cry: from dogma to the Gospel. A factual assessment shows that the early church dogma concerning Christ interpreted the Gospel completely correctly. With impressive sharpness of thought and a fine sense for nuance, the best brains of the early church chiseled out the formula that expresses Christ's mystery as it was experienced by his own disciples and as it must have been expressed so that all possible corruption would be extinguished.

Dogma was born at the baptismal font. It has grown out of the need of Christians to confess whom they believed in. It has hardened, deepened, and matured in defense against all the objections and false doctrines that could be carried into the field against "the faith once and for all handed down to the saints" (Jude 3). Modern scholars are constantly amazed anew by this, that practically everything that our era presented as "new" thoughts concerning Jesus had already been tested, thought through, and rejected by the Christian church in the first few centuries. It has been said, and not without reason, that the early church in its classical confession of a few lines both summarized and preserved all conceivable Christological problems. The creed is a classical masterwork of the type that only can be compared with the great unsurpassed artistic creations.

THE LORD'S SUPPER

The Lord's Supper really deserves its own shepherd's letter. Everyone who apprehended a whiff of spiritual life in the early church must have noticed that we do not rightly understand how to take advantage of the power that the Apostolic Church possessed in its sacramental life. Within these holy means, Christ has placed a power within this world that is capable of unimaginable things if a person believes in it and uses it properly. This power is a mystery that no one can rightly declare. So, it does not really do much to preach about the sacrament. It is better to let them preach themselves, just as they do when a person celebrates them with the right joy and dignity.

So, neither will I speak much about the sacraments in this shepherd's letter, though they have their place in the inheritance of the early church that alone can be compared with the Word's own place. However, I would rather seriously admonish every Christian,

pastor, and layman to let them speak for themselves.

It certainly has great meaning to preach the
Lord's Supper. It is particularly needed in some
places to be said that Jesus "receives sinners and
eats with them." To go to the Lord's Supper
does not mean that a person makes a claim to
be better than others, but that he confesses that
he is a wretched sinner who would have Jesus
as his savior.

To preach concerning the Lord's Supper is,
however, not the best way to a rich and right life
of communion. The Lord's Supper is just one side
of the disciple's association with their Lord. So,
a true communion life cannot exist where there
are not true disciples. The proclamation must
first awaken and lead the way. The Word must
call and enlighten. Therefore, it has with it more
gain for the communion life if one speaks clearly
and sincerely about the love of Jesus for sinners
and the forgiveness of sins in his name, than if
man constantly preaches about the glory of the
Lord's Supper. Naturally, there should also be

instruction on the fifth chief part of the catechism. It shall not happen in isolation but as an attachment to the other aspects of Christianity, without its organized place in conversion and sanctification. People need to be constantly reminded that the Lord's Supper is instituted for all the disciples of Jesus. If a man has resorted to prayer and the Word in an honest longing for salvation, then he should also go forward to receive the gifts at his Lord's table. The Lord's Supper is a means of grace. Everyone who seeks grace not only can but may and ought to make use of it.

That which remains to be said concerning the Lord's Supper, it says better itself. When it is celebrated diligently and with all dignity and the joy-filled solemnity that is found in this encounter with the resurrected One, then it prepares itself a greater place in the heart of the congregation than any zealous preaching can ever give it. Better than any ever so well-meaning pastor who bids the sinner to God and more powerfully than any human admonition binds the heart with their Lord.

If communion attendance seems to drop, a person should therefore rather increase than decrease opportunities to commune. Lutheran church life has suffered hard because people all too seldom get to experience a complete and full Divine Service and receive the pulling power that proceeds from the Lord's table. If the frequency of communion has been good, then the Divine Service has been unnecessarily lengthened on Holy Communion day. The consequence has been that, in turn, people received the custom of absenting themselves when the service of the meal begins. This conflicts with both Scripture and church law. The Scriptures admonish us to stay together just at Holy Communion and "wait for one another" so that the congregation's communion can be preserved. The celebration of Holy Communion can never be its own thing for just those who want to approach the altar on that day. The whole congregation is to be present lifting their hearts to God when Christ visits us. It is really good, right, and salutary that we then all thank

God for his ineffable charity. The Lord's Supper proclaims "the Lord's death until he comes." A person ought to listen to this proclamation just as much as to the day's sermon.

"As often as you eat this bread and drink this cup, you proclaim the Lord's death until he comes" (1 Cor. 11:26). It is precisely this word that perhaps has a particular reality today. Men usually ask—sometimes with a certain impatience—"what tasks church has for them." In the evangelical church we usually do not answer by laying upon them a long list containing every possible form of "spiritual activity." Later I shall try to show that this is not some accident but depends on the innermost aspect of our faith. Here I will only point out one aspect of a task that is often despised and forgotten. This task belongs together with the call of a Christian man. He can proclaim his Lord's death. He can make a very clear and eloquent witness concerning his death and resurrection for his sake. He does this when he in the midst of the congregation goes forward to the Lord's table. This requires a great deal of confessional courage. A young man who goes to communion for the first time after a long time since his confirmation can feel the bewildered looks of his friends like a hail of arrows all about him. A housewife or an honest man who simply enters into "the way" can feel it terribly difficult to take the few steps up to the altar. A sinner, who is all too well conscious of how much has broken in his previous life, is tempted to push and push his communion attendance off for fear of his old antagonists or fellow sinners. In such a case it can help to know: here I am really placed to proclaim my Lord's death. This belongs to the task that my Lord has given me. Just as I shall be a living, singing, praying, and listening participant in every divine service, so I am also called to do my spiritual temple duty. Precisely here I make my contribution according to my Lord's will, and for just that reason I may trust that this will cause my witness to work stronger on my friends and acquaintances than any self-appointed spiritual activity anyone could do.

Naturally, what is great about the Lord's Supper is not what I do or confess. The great thing is that which the Resurrected One does. It far surpasses all that I can fathom or describe. Perhaps his work intervenes the deepest when I do not have any "experience" and do not really feel anything. Sometimes, behind and under all feelings, a hidden work happens where my Lord confirms my faith and gives me more and more of the tested firmness that does not waver in the dry times, and even in life's hardest tests rests on the foundation that we men can neither lay nor destroy.

In this context, perhaps it ought to be said that the service of confession and absolution shall remain the service of confession and absolution, just as the Lord's Supper shall be a whole and complete Lord's Supper. The service of confession and absolution is our church's greatest service of repentance, characterized by soul-searching sorrow and confession of sins. These characteristics shall remain, and a person should not try to give confession a whiff of the eucharistic joy. Yet just so, Holy Communion should not be changed by the character of the service of confession, so confession shall not encroach upon the Lord's Supper. In the Lord's Supper new tones ring. Absolution is given, the Resurrected One visits us, we are guests at the wedding feast who have the bridegroom among us, the gates of Heaven are opened and we hear an echo of the praises sung by seraphim. In the midst of oppression and worries we experience what it means to "be born again to a living hope through the resurrection of Jesus" (1 Pet. 1:3). This tone of victorious jubilee has accompanied the celebration of the Lord's Supper since apostolic times when the disciples broke bread and "received their food with glad and generous hearts, praising God" (Acts 2:46–47). It cannot die away. We need it just as much as the first Christians. And we have just as great a reason to rejoice as they did and do.

THE OFFICE

Modern Christendom would have probably totally forgotten that even the office belongs to the inexhaustible inheritance from the Apostolic Church if scholarship had not so energetically reminded her of it.

The twelve apostles were their Lord's trustees and deputies, dressed in full authority to speak in his name, to forgive sins like him, and to continue his work. In their succession, new men have received the task to be shepherds and teachers in God's congregations. The church is an organism where not all members have the same function. In his church, "God has appointed in the church first apostles, second prophets, third teachers" (1 Cor. 12:28), so that they would have responsibility for the flock and persevere with instruction. So, the office is one of Christ's own institutions, one of the means through which he continues his Word and still speaks and acts on earth.

Now, there is no doubt that the enemy of souls has a particularly good eye for watching those who have been clothed with this office, so alertness and grace are both needed to avoid being caught in his snares. An unconverted pastor is a great opportunity for the enemy of souls. A pastor too can be unconverted. He can be that in a very fine and hidden manner, so that he is both zealous and active without ever at any time experiencing his heart's innermost selfishness and self-confidence as the chief sin that it is. He can also be it in such a coarse manner that it is noticed and awakens offense. When this comes about, the enemy of souls has no greater ally than the pastor's own old Adam. With the old Adam's help, the holy ministry can be changed into something very unholy. The pastor becomes touchy and power hungry. So he guards his prestige instead of gladly bearing Christ's shame. He is a lord (herr)[2] rather than a shepherd. His heart's desire is not the salvation of the souls but his own place among men. The

---

2 Herr Pastor is a term still used in English-speaking Lutheranism for an overly authoritarian pastor.

authority that he receives "to build up and not to break down" then becomes a tool of destruction that breaks down the congregation and embezzles the flock rather than gathering it. It is just as bad if the pastor out of pure consideration for his person does not dare to be a pastor, if he would rather escape being seen in his clergy shirt, if he dulls his Lord's message and becomes an inoffensive say-nothing who enjoys being left alone in peace when he should have rather preached repentance in his Lord's name.

There is just as much egoism in a pastor's fleshly arrogance as in his fleshly modesty. His most dangerous occupational temptation is perhaps these two: on the one hand, preoccupation with himself, wanting to be the center of attention everywhere and have the decisive word, he loves to be first at the smorgasbord and the evening's keynote speaker; and on the other hand, the cowardly indulgence that will not risk his popularity, he is too cautious to say that nothing but faith in Jesus can save an individual and that nothing but God's word can give us this faith—or maybe he only says it once in a while to calm his conscience, yet says it so obscurely or so abstractly that none of his hearers understands that a person can in fact be eternally lost by using Sunday after Sunday as a slow day to practice orienteering or dig in his garden.

A pastor must be simultaneously fearless and unassuming, bold on behalf of his Lord and humble concerning himself, prepared to turn the other cheek when he is exposed for personal injustices, and wholly stubborn when it comes to holding fast to his Lord's Word. He is to make his forehead as hard as a brass ball against the world's insults and at the same time have a heart so sensitive that no one in the congregation can be struck by misfortune or suffer ruin without the pastor carrying his share of the suffering.

So there lies a grim seriousness in Chrysostom's words: *Mirum est si sacerdos salvetur.* "It is a miracle if a priest is saved." The matter is so serious that it is best to immediately be reminded of what the Savior said to his disciples when they began to comprehend how hard it can be to win eternal life. "With man it is impossible, but not with God. For all things are possible with God" (Mark 10:27).

If a man wants to be a pastor he must be it by the power of Christ. If a man is sent to speak on Christ's behalf, then no half measures are possible. A pastor is a slave of Christ. He is mastered by his Lord, driven by his Spirit, filled by the Spirit, filled by the desire to serve his cause. This means also filled with the desire to serve and help the men for whom the Savior gave his life. Only then can the authority be an authority of the Spirit that does not tear down but builds up. This authority does not express itself in the school board or in the ministerium. However, it is perceived stronger in the pulpit. It is noticed that the pastor wants something from his sermon. It is at the same time noticed that he does not seek something for himself. He is the herald who speaks on behalf of his king. So that it awakens the slumbering, comforts the heavy laden, and confirms those who believe.

The pastor has them before his eyes when he prepares his sermon. Their faces have flashed before his inner sight, their worries and temptations have been in his thoughts. It is they that he has thought of and not of his own reputation as a preacher. Constantly anew he has prayed for them and desired that it should please God through this word to kill apathy and kindle the sanctifying flames of faith.

This true authority is always warmhearted and merciful. It does not originate from wounded conceit or personal grudges. Otherwise, it happens often enough that the preacher can be completely tame and gentle so long as he feels popular and is treated with pure friendliness. Only when he is opposed or admonished does he become sharp in his preaching. Such zealousness ought to be rightly called jealousy. It never bears any repentance or living fruit. Anyone can see that the pastor speaks for his own cause and uses the law as a weapon against his litigants. Admonitions do not make an impression if they are not compelled by God's Spirit from a heart of human cowardice that would otherwise be silent but for the sake of love is compelled to speak. So, the pastor ought to be particularly keen to clearly and honestly preach repentance precisely when all men are most friendly and accommodating toward him. Just then he has the greatest opportunity to help them. It is then easiest for them to understand that "it is God who admonishes through us."

Perhaps some brother in the office asks himself anew the question no pastor can escape: have you ever preached without thinking of your reputation? Have you ever proclaimed God's Word only for the sake of the souls, without an afterthought of how you made yourself look, whether you were satisfied with your presentation or went and stepped on your feelings of inferiority?

Before God, this question can only be answered in one way: Father, I have sinned before Heaven and before you. I am no longer worthy to be called your representative. You have entrusted me with the highest of all confidences and entrusted me with the most beautiful of all tasks — and after so many years I still have the same arrogant and self-absorbed heart, hungry for fame and anxious before suffering and trouble.

The pastor who takes his office seriously does not learn to avoid feeling the daily prick of the thorn in his flesh. The old Adam does not die in ordination. He continues to punch us in the face like the angel of Satan he is. However, Christ's miraculous power reveals itself most prominently in that he is capable of using our sins as means of sanctification and our defeats as victories for his cause. When Satan's angel punches me in the face, then it is "to keep me from becoming conceited"(2 Cor. 12:7). Every move of the old Adam becomes a new reason for me to turn my eye to Christ, to keep myself close to him who alone can reconcile my evil heart with God and alone has the power to help a wretched pastor through all of his temptations. Only when I know that it is a great miracle that a pastor is saved, and that I therefore need Christ's atonement and Christ's intercession every minute, only then can I experience the complete depths of the truth that Christ is a real savior for real sinners. So, we do not need to stop at the truth that it is a great miracle that a pastor is saved. We can also say: because I am a pastor, I know that even the greatest sinner can be saved.

———◆———

Among life's most beautiful experiences belongs the joy of being a small member of a greater context, an unmeaningful and quickly forgotten coworker in a great work that lasts when a person himself is long past. A person often encounters the feeling of a strong and beautiful motive among men willing to sacrifice in the ranks of a labor movement, in student unions, or among temperance advocates.

God has made this joy possible for us all in deeper and richer measure when he made us members of the Apostolic Church. No one else's movement of life spans such an immense context, nor counts so many centuries of experience, nor possesses so many martyrs and confessors, nor has fought through such hard opposition, nor has carried so much in the way of immeasurable blessings for the whole of our Western lands, for children and the sick, for women and the elderly, for home and society. When we carry a little child to baptism, that child is incorporated into a society that is thousands of years older than even the state of Sweden. When we open our Bible, we read a writing from Eastern antiquity that still has a living power and is still read in cottages and cited on the lips of people. When we join in confessing the Apostle's Creed, we confess the one truth that has remained unextinguished for two millennia and continues to remain. It is comforting that there is something like this in the world. It is great to be able to fade into the church's immense context that spans more than the whole of our history and contains so infinite an amount of sacrificial will and love. Yet it is still greater to be the little link in this immense context that is encompassed by an eternal love, where he who is the omnipotent Lord of all envelops the most wretched of his servants with such consideration as if he had nothing else to consider. Yet, the very best is that this immense event that applies to millions would have been a reality even if it only applied to a single human soul. Had no one else on earth needed to be saved but myself, God would have still become man and died for my sake. The Gospel would still have been found, someone would have been sent to baptize me and teach me to keep what my Lord commanded. For God wants that all men should be saved, and his Son has been given for us all, no one forgotten, and no one excepted.

II.

INHERITANCE
FROM THE
REFORMATION

JUSTIFICATION BY FAITH

When as an Augustinian monk, brother Martin Luther wrestled with the text of Romans and finally grasped what God's righteousness means, then he found "the key to the knowledge," the key that had been lost for centuries. With amazed eyes he read the Scriptures and understood what he never understood before. Step by step he went further until he saw everything in a new light: what the Gospel is, who

Christ is, what salvation means and how a right Christian life must have been procured.

It can seem peculiar that this key of knowledge could ever be lost within Christianity where the Gospel is read daily. Perhaps though it is not so peculiar. The nature of man is blind when it comes to the Gospel. Luther never tired of emphasizing that natural reason is thoroughly papist. The Gospel demands revelation. It can only be seen with the eyes that are opened by God himself. The doctrine of works has an immediately overwhelming power. It fits completely and fully with the conception that man makes for himself concerning God. God has also written the law in the hearts of the heathen. The notion of right and wrong is innate within us all. The evil conscience is a common experience for all men, and every normal person knows what guilt is. Because we are all created by God, we all have some little perception of the moral law that God instituted for the life of man. When the heart of man begins to seek God, it knows beforehand that there are works that awaken his wrath and other works that please him.

So, man is by nature convinced that the way to God's grace must go through a life that fits with his will. The knowledge of this will can be very dark, but the foundational view is the same: fulfill the law and God will be gracious. Break it, and it will go bad for you.

This doctrine of works is also in Israel and Christianity. It invokes God's own word. Of course, God has said that the wages of sin is death, and he has told us that we ought to be holy just as he himself is holy. So, the prophetic word witnesses to the very same thing that man's heart knew beforehand.

So, it is most natural and popular for all forms of piety to take God's law seriously. The Pharisee is the archetype for this piety that the natural man understands and appreciates. Even if he himself will not comfortably take the harsh path of strict piety to the law, he is convinced that if he should determine to be seriously pious, then he would naturally have something in common with the style of the strict and principled Pharisee. Naturally not the sort of hypocrite that we commonly imagine with the title of Pharisee—typically enough, broad opinion has made itself a completely false picture of the Pharisees and painted them as deceptive frauds who consciously cheated before God. It was just that which the Pharisees did not do. They were infinitely careful with the tenth of mint, cumin, and dill. They knew exactly what expressions a person could use and could not use. They were demonstrably conscientious with their devotional habits. They could travel over land and sea to make a single proselyte, and they seriously thought that the Lord's law was their pride and their joy. In a word, they were the examples of piety in Israel, inheritors of the great awakening that happened in the days of the Maccabees.

That such people could be presented as worse sinners than publicans and whores, that surpasses all that natural reason can fathom. So, it has been common for people in all times to read something else into the Gospel other than what is actually written, and make the Pharisees out to be conscious deceivers. So a person besmirches them, and all the while maintain their own pharisaical notions with good conscience.

The pharisaical piety of the law is the most common of Christendom's distortions. It is ineradicable because it springs from the nature of man himself. It perpetually creates new forms for itself: high church, low church, and unchurch. Even where man opposes Christianity it appears again. The profane humanism shares this basic view wholly and completely: it is man's deeds, his striving and effort that make him worthy and lift him to the divine.

But is it so?

Well, in a certain manner it is so. This really is God's law, revealed by Moses and the prophets, confirmed by Jesus himself: if you want to enter into eternal life, keep the commandments. Be ye perfect as your Father in Heaven is perfect.

Naturally, a man shall live a good, right, merciful, and loving life. He was created precisely for this by God. He has received life from him so that he should live as his child, in communion with him, joyfully, happily, and unconditionally loyal to his will. This is man's purpose: to fear and love, thank and praise, obey and serve his heavenly Father.

Now here comes the problem. No man does this either uncoerced or completely. That the will is rebellious and hostile to God is a grim and inevitable reality. God's own creation has turned against him. "The heart is deceitful above all things, and desperately sick; who can understand it?" (Jeremiah 17:9)

Now it is clear for every piety that has anything to do with the truth of the Bible that this heart that is hostile to God and deviates from him must be changed to truly love God. Man must convert from his evil ways to serve this one, true God. The piety of the law takes this very seriously. The Pharisees feel the law in their five fingers and have in every detail made clear to themselves what they may and may not do. The monk has resolved to turn his back on all earthly joys and live completely for God. And so this piety is encountered in hundreds of modern forms through which it wants to radically break with the world and consecrate his life to work for God's kingdom.

This experience shows two things. It means to change your life. So long as it means an external life change, a man can go a long way with self-discipline and firm principles. A righteous and good pharisee can go a long way, so far as Saul of Tarsus, who was "as to righteousness under the law, blameless" (Phil. 3:6). To be a righteous master, a faithful and honest man, an exemplary member of the congregation, this lies within the human ability.

However, there is one thing that does not change, and that is the heart. It remains a malicious and corrupted thing. It continues to be arrogant, to harbor resentment for the sake of an injustice, to believe all evil about his enemies and long for fame and recognition.

There are constantly new reasons to boast. The heart can be proud of his cross and be pleased with his humility. He can establish worthiness when it asks concerning forgiveness because it happened. He can sit and observe his own devotional practices with delight. And worst of all, it is and remains hostile to God. There is something within the heart that even during all its pious practices is unkind to God, something that feels coerced to pray, something that greedily keeps account of how much it costs him and is always ready to say: now it is enough. This hostility to God is also unfriendly toward people. It looks with greedy envy at the joy of others, there is a lustful pleasure that digs at the faults of others and enjoys the sinful fall of another under the guise of pious concern.

A person can close their eyes to this. The piety of the law must close its eyes to get the accounting together. Herein lies the deceit and hypocrisy. While it gives a tenth of mint, dill, and cumin, it omits "that which is most important in the law, namely justice, mercy, and faithfulness." Naturally not in such a way that a man makes himself guilty of deceit, abuse, and looseness, but precisely through the heart's selfishness, its harsh judgments of others and its inertia and discomfort before God.

An upright heart cannot close its eyes to the truth. When God's own Spirit makes it clear that a person still does not love God above all things, without thought to his own glory, then he bows his heart in a new confession of sin and prays to be completely purified from all sin. Perhaps the fighting soul attempts greater strictness. Brother Martin mortified himself until his health was in jeopardy. His modern brothers or sisters still think of something else, something that must be sacrificed: the midday cigarette, the sweet summer dress, the little savings of capital, or the intended engagement.

However, the heart is not changed. It remains what the Bible calls the flesh and our fathers named original sin. The old man is and remains the same. He can be forced to behave as a Christian, but he always does it under duress and resistance.

Here we catch a glimpse of what is actually the problem of life: how a thoroughly egotistical man with flesh that is hostile to God shall be a child of God.

Sham solutions immediately offer themselves. Can God not forgive? Can God not overlook when I myself want to be his? Or, will God not continue to give me power to overcome this evil heart even if ever so gradually? Certainly, he will create a clean heart within me if I sincerely ask him for it? Or finally, there must be some means of repentance that changes everything? If I have not yet encountered it, then perhaps some new spiritual movement can mediate it for me. . .

An upright heart cannot make use of any of these sham solutions. It knows that God forgives. However, it also knows that faith's essence is unbroken communion with God. I shall not only ask God for forgiveness, I shall also unite with him and live completely for him. Yet here comes the unreasonable thing. My heart is so full of malaise and inertia that it cannot be completely united with God. Could I then cheat and note that I am never better, and still comfort myself saying that God lets the odd be even? The heart declines to go in for such a resolution. The conscience knows all too well that God condemns sin within me.

Just as little does the hope that the heart will gradually be purified find fulfillment. I pray and pray for it, and while I pray, I begin to think of my contemptible enemies or that fatal surety bond or the lost door key—and immediately I can see that my heart is just the same.

So, the last hope appears, the most fraudulent of them all: that some spiritual movement will come or there will be some spiritual experience that changes everything. It is this hope that drives men into monasteries or into the arms of strange heresies. For a short time, a person might be able to hide his evil heart behind a gala parade of new feelings and impressions. However, the new becomes old, and then the old heart is there again, and it is completely the same.

Martin Luther had come that far when he rediscovered the key to knowledge. One day it became clear to him that neither he nor his contemporaries had ever understood what the Bible meant by God's righteousness. In the obvious manner of the law's piety, they had thought that it was the righteousness that God demanded of us. However, here it spoke of "the righteousness from God" and that God "makes the ungodly righteous," and this "without works." It was written that God imputes this righteousness without asking after his law, that it was a gift, that it was attained through faith in Jesus, in such a way that through his obedience many would stand as righteous.

Thereby, the key that opens up the all the locks of Scripture was rediscovered. If a person has not understood this, he cannot fathom what the Gospel really means. The Gospel is God's resolution of that which seems to be an unresolvable problem, how an ungodly man can be

a child of the God who is incorruptibly righteous. Human nature is helplessly selfish. It
is just as impossible to clean a human heart of
selfishness as it is to clean the black color from
a piece of coal. God is incorruptibly righteous.
It is just as impossible to unite the selfishness of
man with the holiness of God as it is to build a
summer villa in a stream of lava or sit down in
the middle of the sun.

Just as fully God loves every little selfish
man, loves him with a deep and eternal love.
And because there is no way upon which man
should climb up to God, and no possibility for
the selfish human insect to endure the presence
of God's righteous fire, so God has found a way
down to man and created a possibility for sinners to live in God's presence.

This God has done through the incarnation,
by himself becoming a man. He took on the
form of a servant and came to us in the appearance of a man. He received the worst conceivable reception. He came to his own and his own
did not receive him. He encountered a hate that

only a fallen world can show to its true Lord. However, he repaid all this hate with kindness. He blessed when he was cursed. He fulfilled all that his fallen children were obligated to do. He atoned for what they had broken. He bore their guilt as his own, he let himself be condemned to death and taste the most extreme consequences of their evil and fall.

All this he did in the form of the Son. This is the Son's mystery: God was in Christ reconciling the world to himself (2 Cor. 5:19). The law that God placed as a wall between his kingdom and evil had up until then been Satan's greatest asset. The judgment over evil must stand fast. Rebellion and the evil will, low-mindedness and the contempt for God's Spirit have no place in God's kingdom and shall never slip in. For just this reason, the sinner's situation is so desperate. His heart's resistance to God and his being's selfishness shut him out from God's presence. It is so according to the foundation of existence, according to the demand of eternal righteousness.

Only in Christ has the inconceivable miracle happened, that which our reason only ever partially comprehends in piecemeal. God himself has fulfilled all righteousness when he walked about as a man among men and bore his brother's burden. He suffered innocently for the guilty. Christ died for our sins. God redeemed his children with his own blood. God no longer credits man with their sins. He showers them with Christ's righteousness. So, he can make the ungodly righteous.

All this now happens through faith. Faith in Christ means the heart's mysterious union with Christ. The man became a member in Christ's body, a branch in his vine, a stone in his temple building. All that Christ did, suffered, fought for, and won is now his. The debt note is nailed fast to the cross. Instead of the well-earned reward for his egoism, the amazed man receives all the blessedness that Christ alone has deserved. Paradise opens for the thief, and even the prisoners in hell had the Gospel proclaimed to them.

So, there is only one basis upon which a man who knows all too well that he has a malicious and corrupted heart can be a child of God. This basis is called Jesus Christ—and another foundation can no one lay. Only in faith's mysterious union with Christ is the sinner united with God himself. Only here, under the Savior's pierced hand is it possible for the sinner to step before God with unclouded childish trust and feel his righteous fire as the flames of love they actually are.

But how is it then with works? Should we remain in sin that grace should abound all the more?

The question is already asked in the New Testament, and emphatically rejected as unreasonable. When, in his infinite mercy, God allows the whole of the atonement to depend on this alone: to believe in Jesus, and then in his wisdom he also made it so that faith could never be inactive. This sanctifying faith means a union with Christ, a communal life with the Savior. To have forgiveness is to have Christ.

Yet in the same moment as Christ is in a man's heart, there is also a fight against the flesh and all its deeds. He who believes has within him the Spirit who never compromises. So, he also has a lifelong fight before him. "For the desires of the flesh are against the Spirit, and the desires of the Spirit are against the flesh, for these are opposed to each other" (Gal. 5:17). However, a man does not need to carry this fight in order to be righteous. He fights this fight because he is righteous. In Christ, he already participates in this full righteousness. All is forgiven, even his unrepentant, selfish heart. All his remaining sinful inheritance is drowned in a sea of grace. His childishness does not depend on him attaining some sort of victory, but that he gives himself and the whole of his lost cause into the hands of Jesus. For just this reason there is a victory. Just when man no longer fights desperately to make himself righteous but fights against sin because he loves his Savior and "makes it his aim to please him" (2. Cor. 5:9), just then it shows that "the grace of God has appeared, bringing salvation for all people, training us to renounce ungodliness and worldly passions, and to live self-controlled, upright, and godly lives in the present age" (Titus 2:11–12).

This is the key to knowledge that is called justification by faith. If a person finds it, then the whole context of Scripture opens in overwhelming power and clarity. A person sees the law's great meaning: to discipline an external innocence, and to be a pedagogue for Christ. A man also sees the law's impotence when it comes to making man righteous before God. A person finally understands the overwhelming meaning of Christ. He comprehends what a fundamental mistake he committed when one saw him only as an example, a lawgiver, a guide to works of love. Were he not more than that, then we would be all lost. For who has followed this example? Who has lived according to the law of the Sermon on the Mount? Who has actualized his love? "But now the righteousness of God has been manifested apart from the law, although the law and the prophets bear witness to it—the righteousness of God through faith in Jesus Christ for all who believe. For there is no distinction: for all have sinned and fall short of the glory of God, and are justified by his grace as a gift, through the redemption that is in Christ Jesus" (Romans 3:21–24). This is the chief summary of the Gospel. It is the key to all the mysteries of Scripture.

It is this inheritance from the Reformation, set in a single formula. This key is nothing for us to lose. The doctrine of justification by faith is and remains the article with which the church stands and falls.

From this article a man can then come to a right view of both man and the life of man. The reformers had already seen this, and what they have seen and learned at that time should be even more real than ever today.

THE VIEW OF MAN

First comes the view of man. What the Reformation means here would be immediately clear for every man, if ignorance concerning the foundational concepts of the Lutheran faith were not so great as they unfortunately are even in our Lutheran land.

What does the Gospel concerning justification by faith mean today? In Stalin's and Sartre's era, in the era of slave camps and atom bombs? A superficial observer first thinks that the message of the forgiveness of sins for the sake of Jesus should have absolutely nothing to say in this age of human animals. Yet, all the materialistic theories concerning our kinship to predators and parasites, all the claims concerning the fight for existence as the foundational law of life, seem to have proven to be as equally appalling in convincing ways.

It probably speaks for itself. The strange thing is only that a person does not see that what is normally enlisted as evidence for materialism's view of man can just as well be used as confirmation that the Gospel is right in its view of man. The conception of man that really finds it difficult to stand before the witness of reality is profane humanism. The whole of this belief in man that held up the culture of optimism at the turn of the century has received a harsh refutation. It is quite simply not true that mankind possesses much goodwill and common sense so that it only needs a little organization and illumination for progress to be assured.

The two world wars have taught us that the result can be the direct opposite when man organizes the powers to do what in fact exists in the nature of man. The new ideology has taught us that there is an inexhaustible storehouse of egoism and suspiciousness among mankind and that they can be organized to carry out virtually any crime. Psychology has taught us that it is precisely the dark drives in man that often determine his actions. Modern literature quite emphatically claims that man's basic instinct is egoism, a hunger for power, and lust, that everything that daily happens in a home or in a circle of friends, at an office or within a political party, is dictated by pure greed for money, to assert one's self, or to satisfy sexual drives.

It ought to be rather apparent that such people cannot provide stable support for happy societal development, and just as little for relationships between people and classes characterized by tolerance, consideration, and a willingness to sacrifice.

So, Christianity has been shown to be right in its realistic conception of man. That which at the turn of the century was characterized by radical circles as a dark view of man's nature has proven to be naked fact. That despite this a person so seldom sees that the Gospel has proven right, this is partially because man does not want to see it. Yet it can also be because the little bit man knows concerning the Gospel is scavenged from such muddied sources.

Liberal theologians make up one of these muddied sources. They have long ago been overcome by science, but in the popular conscience they still rule in their area. Their view of man is a twin brother to cultural optimism. The two wholeheartedly share a naïve faith in man. Their spokesmen deny both the devil and original sin. They do not have any understanding for the fundamental truth that comes from the background of the Gospel: that this world is fallen, that evil is an appalling reality, and that man without Christ is hell-bent to ruin. Above all, these liberal theologians are responsible for causing this war with all these miseries to become a catastrophe for so many people's belief in God. If a person has been blinded to the fact that Satan also works in history, then he must ascribe all evil to God's account, and then faith in a loving God becomes impossible to keep. However, this god that man then rejects is the god of liberal theologians, not the Gospel.

The other faulty source is the Christian narrative literature that has its source of inspiration in Anglo-Saxon revival piety. This too has a very un-Lutheran view of man. Certainly, it accounts for the power of evil and the fearsome context of sin. It can describe life without Christ in the harshest of harsh terms, in a manner that does not fit well with Christian faith in creation. Through a sudden conversion all is so changed that the villains become saints and the old Adam is completely conquered. This scheme has been criticized in literary circles as a gross perversion of facts. Lutheranism can add to this criticism with the whole weight of its experience. Even God's saints are sinners. Their Lord may have just as much patience with them as with his first disciples. A Lutheran description of man dares to speak very clearly about the faults of Christians precisely because it can speak just as clearly about Christ's atonement, and knows both that grace is enough and that amid all human frailty faith is still active in love.

The third faulty source is bad plans for Christian instruction.[1] Often these try to make something like the Sermon on the Mount into the chief source for instruction of the Christian faith and believe that the law in the Sermon on the Mount can be applied as a rule of life to everyone with just a little goodwill. This

---

1 Here Bo Giertz specifically attacks a plan for Christian instruction designed for the Swedish public school system in 1919 when he was in school himself.

misconception is the reason that we hear so many today claim that Christianity is "impossible to practice" or "unrealistic." They have discovered that it does not work for them to turn the other cheek, and experience has taught them that it is not at all the love of the Sermon on the Mount that determines the societal life of people. That Jesus did not say any such thing either is something that has not dawned on them.

What really shows itself to be unrealistic is the idealism that does not take the radical reality of evil into account. It is unrealistic to believe that humanity can simply solve its problems with the help of intelligence and the altruistic intentions included in our nature. Modern literature has this quite right when it so ruthlessly reveals all the cowardice and evil that exist in fallen humanity. Modern literature would be completely right, however, if at the same time it also had eyes for the good that is found in mankind and even in the midst of mankind's humiliation shows that man is created by God. A person is also able to correct himself and show mercy. A man can show both friendship and love for elders. He has the atoning gift of humor and is able to do great things when at times he is motivated by a genuine and warm enthusiasm. Perhaps all this is stained by his egoism, yet it is still there as a fragment of the law that the Creator wrote upon his heart. He can also be God's child. He can be saved. This does not mean that he becomes a saint free of sin, capable of demonstrating in the large storefront window of the Pharisees. However, he is a struggling man in whom God's Spirit constantly exposes, forgives, and binds the forces of egotism. A man who practices small everyday acts of tenderness, consideration, fidelity to duty, and patience.

To not want to see any of this is to distort reality. It often appears that a good deal of modern literature does not want to see this. It paints man's innate sinfulness with an almost sadistic glee that seeks out every bit of ugliness within us, but it does not do it from mercy, or in the manner of a *seelsorger* seeking to condemn and forgive evil, but rather so that it should be accepted as the whole and final truth of man.

It is very strange that in culturally radical circles people often stand with such uncritical admiration and awe before such hard-boiled literature. It is actually the most pessimistic critique of the old belief in progress and worldly idealism that can possibly be conceived. It seems as if the Western Christendom is about to end up with a view of man that is just as one-sided and false as the idealistic idylls. It is a step forward if we no longer imagine that the nature of man is good. It is useful to see evil such as it is. However, nothing is won if we accept this evil as the definitive and unchangeable reality. Man is a sinner, this is true. However, we may not make man into an animal nor into an irresponsible bundle of instincts. The truth is neither the unrealistic optimism that believes everything sorts itself nor the similarly unrealistic cynicism that says everything is crass demands and dirty selfishness. We also have a third possibility: our everyday confessional Lutheranism. For us who

rediscovered this or always confessed it, there is
no surprise that things have gone as they have
gone. To speak of the goodness of man was a
myth; Christianity has always known this, both
from Scripture and from its own experience.
However, we also know that it is precisely these
men with all their lechery, their ridiculous pet-
tiness, their cruelty, and cowardice that God
loves. God has not abandoned them. He knows
their being and their deeds far better than any
hard-boiled author, but he still looks upon them
with infinite mercy. He has not isolated himself
from them, not withdrawn, but on the contrary
descended to them and in an inconceivable sacrifice dove down to the bottom of their dirtiness
and misery and atoned for it all in order to make
them his children again.

It is this view of man that is truly human,
the real meaning of human. We are not blind to
any of man's faults. However, at the same time,
we also see that in the midst of man's humiliation man is created by God and loved by God.
He is created by God, and therefore he always

possesses some splash of true love, a sense for right and justice, of goodwill and good humor. A man can already make good use of these if he understands how to make God's law applicable in the right way, to awaken a response in the heart. But for this every man is loved by the God who gave his own Son for his sake. He has opportunity to commune with God and thereby receive new life. If we want to see what a man is worth in the eyes of God, then we must look to the cross in Golgotha. The cross is the seal of man's worth. God so loved the world... He has loved the millions upon millions crowded upon busses and trams, who mill about in factories, who go to work between stone fences or struggle in the rough seas between the skerries. So much is each and every one of them worth to him.

This Christian view of man is absolutely realistic. It sees man such as he is and notes matter-of-factly that he is a sinner, an egoist, an impulsive person with lecherous and cruel instincts. It also sees God's love for man. It sees what has in fact happened in history: Jesus Christ has died for us egoists. Finally, it sees also clearly and factually what happens when the Crucified encounters one of these sinners. It knows from manifold experience that something new comes with Christ. The old man remains, all the old instincts move within him, but there has also come a spiritual power that fights against sin and hinders it from taking control. Where this power grabs hold of man after man, then the whole structure is changed and the whole of culture is transformed. This too is lived experience and a realistic view of history.

LIFE IN SOCIETY

The Lutheran view of man that is both realistic and merciful, both lacking delusion and full of possibility, is contrasted with a closely related view of societal life and our duties in this world.

For the piety of the law, it is normally self-evident that a citizen's daily work life is of less importance than exclusively religious occupations or preoccupations. If a man wants to live in devotion to God, then it must happen outside the framework of common gainful employment. A man has to become a monk or hermit, a pastor or deacon, a soldier of salvation or at least a Sunday school teacher.

When Luther rediscovered the key of knowledge, he also discovered the falseness and egocentricity in this mindset. It is no less selfish to live in service of salvation than to live as a slave to money. The monk is just as occupied with what is best for him as any innkeeper. Luther saw through all the pious invention behind which the old man hides his desire to think of himself, speak of himself, and do well for himself. He sensed the old Adam behind the tonsure and habit, but also behind the grey coats of the schwarmerei[2] with their downcast faces and godly sighing. He saw the perversion

---

2 Schwarmerei was a term Luther used for various groups of radicals who thought they had direct communication with the Holy Spirit. Some of these groups were Anabaptists, and

and wickedness in this: that man finds himself in mortification and religious exercises that God never commanded and does these instead of serving his neighbor as God really commanded. Instead of loving his brother and attempting to be a joy and benefit for him, he lives for his own pleasure in his self-appointed religious exercises.

Now in light of justification by faith everything finds its right place: both religious exercises and the daily job. Only one thing is needed for a right relationship between God and man: a right faith. This unites us with Christ, it makes us righteous before God and at the same time active in love. God works this faith through his means of grace. So it is both necessary and right to be a faithful church attender, one who hears, prays, studies, and receives Communion. A living Christianity cannot be found where a man does not stand

---

led peasant revolts. The idea behind the word is a picture of bees swarming with no order.

under the impact of the Word. It is through the divine service and devotional life that God kindles faith and preserves it with his power. However, this is thoroughly God's work, not our accomplishment. Devotions, prayer, edification, self-examination, and recollection are not valuable in that we should do something that is purer or more pious than our daily work. Even our worship and prayer need forgiveness. So, a man can neither be more holy, sanctified, or better by filling his whole life with prayers and worship. Everything should be done in its place and in its time. The means of grace must be used or faith dies. Individual devotions are indispensable; without it the work of grace in our hearts goes stale. The Sunday service should be celebrated, and the worship life be kept in honor, otherwise congregational community is lacking. As God's children we have a right to rejoice with hymns of praise and all pomp and circumstance before his altar. However, if we should then ask what we can do now for our Lord and how he wants these forces he has awakened within us to be used, then he does not demand anything remarkable. Neither fasting nor pilgrimages, neither hair shirts nor homely and unfashionable clothing, neither tonsures nor hair buns are to be the signifiers of our Christianity. Neither does God demand purely "religious activity," nor purely pious literature and music or never-ending games of strictness. God does not need our services. However, all around us we find our fellow man who needs us. The whole of our daily life at home or business, in social work, at the hospital, and in schools we hear the cry for our attention and work. Here Christian love has an inexhaustible field of activity. Here, among precisely these people who are in our closest surroundings, God bids us our best within our places of work, and with the whole of our being to try and be a blessing to them. Here lie the good works and expectations which God has "prepared beforehand that we should walk in them." Here the fruits of faith grow and here man is sanctified in a right way when he takes care of the difficulties and bears the burdens that all daily duties lay upon him.

So, a Christian never needs to seek a cross by imposing particular deprivations upon himself. The cross he is to have waits for him in everyday life. There he receives occasion for the asceticism that is useful and necessary for him. It is self-appointed piety to remove oneself from the world and turn away from marriage and from the common work, from common food and clothing. Such "only serves to nourish the heart of flesh." The ascetism that God offers consists of those times in everyday life that a person fights his sour mood and lazy incompetence, that he has patience with unpleasant people, that he is good to elders when they once again become children, and that he does not get bothered when another receives thanks and praise where he has done most of the work. It is in such tests that a person has occasion to discipline and kill the old Adam. It happens in a diligent and unassuming earthly work. There our flesh is put to death, there our faith is tested, there we learn to trust in God's help.

This Lutheran view of the call or vocation has meant infinitely much for our cultural development.[3] It has made everyday life a service before God and faithfulness in the smallest things a holy duty and a joy at the same time. On that point there is a marked difference between the Lutheran north and the old core of Roman Catholic countries in the south of Europe. The Lutheran knows that it is his duty as a Christian to be immeasurably honorable in his business, careful with his money and his duties toward society, honest and caring in all his work. In the areas of the "old church revival,"[4] even the

---

3 Speaking of the cultural development in Sweden with a work ethic that can still be seen in German and Swedish communities around the world, especially in places like northern Minnesota, for instance.

4 The "old church revival" (gammalkyrkliga väckelsen) was a late eighteenth- and nineteenth-century revival led chiefly by Henric Schartau (1757–1825). In many ways this was an attempt to hold on to Orthodox Lutheranism in the face of Moravian influences through the pietist school of Halle, and even Methodism. Its doctrine and practice, with an emphasis on sacramental church life and the importance of the office

enemies of the revival recognized this matter. In noble estates and in liberal bourgeois homes a man might speak ill of "readers,"[5] but when they want a gardener or maid, they are happy to get someone who belongs to the "old church." Then a person knows they can leave the safe unlocked and that the workday will not be wasted with gossip.

The evangelical view of work is often misunderstood. Sometimes a person hears it said that citizenship itself is a worship and that one can be a good Christian by being honorable and diligent in his work. This is not a Lutheran

---

of the ministry, therefore in many ways is born from the same concerns that shaped the Lutheran Church Missouri Synod through early influences such as Walther and Löhe. Because this movement was counter to the rationalism of the time, it too was labeled as "pietist" even if it was more a reaction against what English-speaking Lutherans have learned to call pietism through the influence of Walther.

5 The old church revivals in Sweden developed into somewhat of a sect whose members were often called "readers" for their habit of reading Scripture often. English slang equivalents may be "Bible-thumpers," "Jesus freaks," "born agains," "evangelicals," or in Lutheran circles, the ever-present "pietist." However, none of these really fits the mold.

understanding but the direct opposite. It is a new edition of the Pharisaical religion of the law or the medieval doctrine of works. It means, of course, that one believes honest everyday work is a good deed, by which one fulfills the law and serves God's pleasure. It is just as bad to believe in the sacrifice of the Mass or monkish vows. It means just as much hypocrisy as Pharisaical righteousness. A man pleases himself with external morals and ignores the inner reality of the heart, the feelings toward an obnoxious coworker or his petty words in family circles. A man replaces the great commandment of love with a selection of the paragraphs in the constitution or a middle-class code of conduct. He certainly gives to the state what belongs to the state—or at least some of it—but he does not give to God what belongs to God. There is neither faith in Christ nor the forgiveness of sins. Faith does not come from success in business or from a well-done work at home. Faith comes from preaching. So, a life without the means of grace can never be a Christian life. The faith that God wants to give us through the Word can never be replaced with the services that we plan to give to God through an honorable everyday life. This is not Lutheran, rather a worldly doctrine of works that says: work is my way of serving God.

One such distortion of the doctrine of vocation we have already talked about. It is the ancient delusion that it must necessarily be more pious to be an evangelist than to be a nanny, and that God must look with great pleasure on those who are active in a church organization and sometimes hold small observations, more than on those who only "keep a home or attend to their work."

Now it can certainly be a person's call to go in a way that departs from the normal citizen's life. Such a call must be obeyed without any excuse. It is a very serious thing if there is a shortage of deacons, deaconesses, pastors, or missionaries. It shows that there must be several men and women among us who are disobedient to God's call, and to this day do something different than obey the call into service of the Word and church that God has given them. Their everyday life is not regarded as high in the eyes of God as the churchly office they rejected. All work is certainly of the same worth before God, if one really goes his way in faith and lets himself be led where God will lead. If one does this, then every work is just as holy, just as churchly, just as spiritual, but not otherwise.

Lutheran teaching emphatically asserts that it is not necessary to find some "religious activity" in order to "give one's life completely to God." Devoted, true Christian life is a prayer life, worship life, and communion life, and beyond that a homelife and a work life. A living Christianity does not need to show itself in that a person begins to keep lectures on the Christianization of the homelife. It shows itself far better in that a person begins home devotions. Conversion does not show itself in that a person collects new duties, but in that one accomplishes the old duties in a new way. Faith does not take

I belong to Christ
all that needed
INHERITANCE FROM THE REFORMATION 139
Ecclesiastes 2:24

a man away from work and home, not out into new associations and companies, but first and foremost deeper into the duties he already has as a member of his family and with gainful employment. It is and remains as Luther has taught us: the true saints look very small in the eyes of the world. Their hands are callous from coarse everyday work, their time is occupied with trivial chores, and their silently done great deeds are not suitable for some sensational witness in a general meeting. They do not see their saintly glory in the mirror. They require a lot of forgiveness and suffer from weakness. Yet they have known their Lord and loved him. Yet all around them there has grown up a generation that cannot doubt that God lives.

———

It is these small and faithful deeds in everyday life that our society so badly needs today. A vacuum has arisen through de-Christianization in work life too. Materialism teaches people that they should live for progress. The hope of a better world should give meaning to the work effort. Yet the work becomes all the more mechanical and soul killing, and world developments give less and less hope for an earthly paradise. So, a man seeks the meaning of life in free time and entertainment. Work becomes a forced evil that a man has to subject himself to so he can get money for leisure.

At the same time development requires increased work effort. Progress can only come through increased production, and increased production costs more work. We need willing and talented hands that do not tire, do not botch the job, and do not let go. It is therefore all the more serious that there seems less spontaneous joy in work in modern society. People long to get away from work. A person routinely handles it without satisfaction, and a person defends himself with horror at the thought that the pace of the work needs to be further increased.

Modern society seems to have very little opportunity to overcome this evil. People try with small means of killing the pain: They buy stereos and play dance music. They hope for shorter work weeks or longer vacations. The individual man is still not helped until he receives a new love for the actual work. He must get something that makes the long work-day into something better than a necessary evil.

It is here that the Lutheran view of work can be a liberating discovery for a modern man who continues to lose the meaning of life because he continues to lose joy in work. The Gospel teaches a person two things he needs to learn: it is precisely this work that is worship of God, a good deed that God looks at with plea-sure when he does it with faith in him and in love for his fellow man, and that it is just these difficulties that he has to overcome that are the best means for his sanctification.

Naturally, it is of little help if this is treated as a theoretical teaching. That which helps man is the Gospel itself, that is to say the encounter with the Resurrected One himself who comes to us and bears our burdens. When all is for-given and encompassed in an infinite love, then even the problem of work is resolved. The heart learns to understand that the meaning of life is to love just as unconditionally as one himself is loved. A man discovers that God's will is just this, that a man shall now live for his brother and that this true worship during the everyday moments consists of a man just doing his daily work joyfully, faithfully, and unselfishly. Here one enters into the creative work of God. Here one is present to present the gifts through which God feeds and clothes his children. Everyone does their part, all are needed, and all are just as highly regarded and loved in the eyes of God. It does not matter if a person stands and packs boxes or sits at a desk, if a person cares for small children or makes new machines. Everything is part of the great work through which God keeps the home together, builds up society, secures the earthly harvest for us men, and makes it more tolerable to live on this earth.

Perhaps some say that a man can have this view of creating work even if he does not believe. Naturally, this is true in the individual case. However, there is reason to believe thatthe great masses of people will only take this view through faith. Experience teaches this. There is actually more joy at work in a village that is characterized by the "old church culture" than there is in the milieu of a de-Christianized big city. This is not because of any benefit of country life. Modern man usually tries to deny those; he would rather flee to the city. It depends on an actual perspective. The Christian sees work in light of the Gospel. It is a service before God. It both serves man's best interest here on earth and fosters their own soul for eternity. A person does it responsibly and for just that reason it is interesting. It is included in God's plans. God himself guarantees that it is not in vain.

If a person does not see God, everything appears differently. It is a small comfort in boredom that my work effort may have some benefit for humanity in the long run. The secularized man who believes this life is the only one he has will not sacrifice himself for an uncertain future. He wants to enjoy the fruit of his labor himself.

The whole of life stands in an inconspicuous and monotonous service that appears to him as nearly a failed life. Work is a necessary evil that he can never give his heart and best efforts to.

The great aspect of the Lutheran view of vocation lies in precisely this association of law and gospel. The earthly work is both a great gift and a useful instruction. No one can value work higher than a Lutheran, and no one can see more clearly how unpleasant and laborious it can be. The doctrine of the call is not blue-eyed romanticism, nor an unrealistic doctrine saying that it is always a joy to work. It is both a strict and merciful truth that man must eat his bread by the sweat of his brow, but it is also precisely in this everyday toil that the world despises that God has placed a blessing that comes in the day when a man does his work in faith. Work has always been monotonous and heavy. We are all tempted to think that we cannot stand doing the same thing for a long day of work. An old, habitual work can only be renewed when an old heart is constantly renewed, when prayer for forgiveness ascends anew, when an old sinner is once again surprised that God has not tired of forgiving and that he really can have patience with us. He who so experiences God's patience, he may himself have patience to bear his work. He daily receives his work anew from God's hand. Here I am placed, here I may serve God, here I can do the good for men that God wants me to do.

This needs to be preached as an aspect of justification. It needs to be made concrete and living. People need help to see what their everyday life actually means, that even this is a place for an encounter with God, where he disciplines and fosters us and where God's love flows out into the world through our hands when we faithfully serve him in a very small thing.

Now the same thing also has another side that may not be forgotten. It is not enough to teach the individual the right view of work. In this context it is the right place to say to a Christian:

You are placed here. Do your best. However, if this is all that a person says, then that person ends up speaking contrary to God and his Word.

It is not only to do one's service in society that is already given. It is also to form this society as sensibly and mercifully as possible. A Christian also serves his brother by working for a just society where the burdens and benefits of life are distributed as fairly as possible.

This too belongs to the inheritance of the Reformation, though the churches of the Reformation have not always seen this. Luther also received from Scripture a powerful overview concerning the whole of societal life. He saw how the whole of our existence in this world is determined by the immense measure of force between the Creator and corrupting powers. First and foremost, this fight has a religious side. It deals with the salvation of the soul. There the fight is carried out with the Gospel. There the goal is the forgiveness of sins through faith in Christ. However, the fight also has a more profane side. The great rebellion against God that threw this world into misery and suffering stretches itself over all areas of life. It works again in both nature and society. Evil powers work everywhere to destroy the order that God has established in creation. The work of evil also takes form in dirty housing, children with tuberculosis, exhausted mothers, economic impoverishment, and irresponsible sexual behavior. Against this God fights with all the good powers he incorporated into his creation. Where God's will is realized the result is social justice, happy homes, secure livelihood and employment, as well healthy and happy people.

Now this fight continues in large part within the realm of the first article. The law that is needed here is also placed in the conscience. It can be understood and respected even if one does not understand Christ and his work. Even where men do not fathom and do not recognize that they are created by God, they are still his work. Without recognizing it themselves, God works in their lives in a thousand different ways. He is present in their reaction against injustices and lies. He lives in their affection and concern for their neighbors. He drives them to do that which is right and merciful at home and in society, at the hospital and in the courts, in nurseries and schools. However, man encounters Satan's tracks in every aspect of society. Sometimes the satanic perversion of creation is almost the only thing a man sees. This does not stop good seed from lying in good earth under the thistles, seed that can grow and bear fruit where one least expects it.

When it comes to justice and good societal order, God can also work through men who do not confess his name. It is a part of his good providence, and providence has never needed faith to be active. So, neither does it need any correct confession of faith in order that a man can be a tool of God's will in social contexts. A Christian has no right to demand such a confession of faith as a condition that he should participate in social tasks or support them in their work. Here it comes to obedience to the law in its "first use," thus as a curb against injustice, abuse, and arbitrariness. It is completely unjustified to say that such things are of no value because they are not united with a true and saving faith in the Lord Christ. Certainly, it is right that from an eternal point of view it does not help a man to escape a toothache and be able to live in decent housing — "for what will it profit a man if he gains the whole world and forfeits his soul?" (Matthew 16:26). Yet it is equally God's will that poverty be fought and plague relieved. The rich man should have thought of Lazarus, and the priest should have thought about the man on the side of the road who had fallen into the hands of robbers. God is the friend of widows, and defender of the fatherless, a refuge for all creation and an enemy of injustice. No one has a right to despise this work because it does not always lead to salvation. Salvation is God's thing. Man shall in any case do his thing so that during the time his neighbor lives here on this earth, his neighbor will be able to have it as tolerable as possible. The second article does not repeal the first, even if it sometimes looks as if the Christian himself believed it.

It belongs to Luther's greatness that he was so intensively focused on confessing justification by faith and at the same time had such a clear view of the contents of the first article. Few others have taught us like Luther to understand that God also cares for our bodies, that he can also use those who do not believe to carry the voice of mercy, and that he established authorities precisely so that there would be tolerable living conditions here on earth. He has also taught us to distinguish between the spiritual and the worldly kingdoms, between church and state. The church lives by the second and third articles. She shall preach the Word and give eternal life. She shall not lord it over and write laws for life on earth. This is society's job. It belongs to the first article and has responsibility for earthly welfare. It has the law and the judiciary at its disposal to keep order with power. The church, however, moves hearts to believe, she gives men new birth and teaches them to love. Just in this way she also serves society. She fights egotism in our hearts and sets the powers in motion that make mercy and love not succumb in the hard fight against selfishness.

The church's duty in society is first and foremost to proclaim and represent God's law. It is not sufficient to speak about love's disposition. God also demands deeds of love. That we should love each other, everyone that has heard a small crumb of Christian proclamation knows that. It is not as certain that he has ever thought about how love should show itself when a man sells his old car, when a person is attacked in the newspapers or when there is not enough money at home. This has been preached too little concerning right and wrong in marriage, on the farm, at the factory with employers and employees, maids and housewives. And yet it is just here that God's law meets man. Here a man is daily placed before God in the choice between his will and the devil's. On these points, modern proclamation is usually too cautious, very taciturn, or very vague. Luther was not this.

He could speak out. The fathers of Lutheran orthodoxy and awakening could do this too. In these eras a person knew that the table of duties also belonged to God's Word. Unfortunately, this has now disappeared from both catechesis and preaching as well as from common consciousness. It is a fatal deficiency if we no longer can proclaim God's good and gracious will in questions of different works, professions, and positions. The task is inconceivably hard. It does not do to repeat what Luther has said. He had thought through his era's societal problems and set the German princely states and the late Middle Ages' middle class in the light of God's Word. We live in a completely different society and must find the answers of Scripture to completely different questions.

One such proclamation of the law has first and foremost as its task to give simple and clear tutorials in elementary moral truths. It means to expose egotism and irresponsibility even in every day's most ingrained habits. It can apply to such simple and common things like parents regarding their children as cheap labor or that children exploit their parents. It needs to be spoken simply, warmheartedly and biblically concerning a housemother's care for her servant girl's comfort, about a Christian farmhouse, and about an employer's responsibility for everyone he has in his service. Perhaps there is also occasion at a family ceremony or after a childcare meeting to speak about how bad it is when parents drive their children to the dance halls because they never let them have their friends at home, or when they compel young people to wait for marriage because they themselves do not feel old enough to retire from farming and have never thought that it could possibly work to have a married son as a farmhand. There are many such questions that ought to be questions of conscience, but never are if the *seelsorger* does not in all seriousness put them in light of the great commandment that one should love his neighbor as himself.

[handwritten: *soul sorter*]

It often happens that the community leaders turn to their pastor when it comes to clearing up difficulties that exceed their own abilities. This can mean childcare stories that no one else is able to sort out. It can entail difficulties in caring for the poor wards that do not allow themselves to be resolved by a ruling of the authorities. It can mean persuading an old grandma to overcome her prejudices and move to the nursing home, or it can be a matter of brokering peace between neighbors or reconciling a tenant and his landlord. It sometimes means unpleasant and thankless tasks. It can demand a lot of time and turn work plans upside down. And then the priest ought to be thankful that he in this way may make a social effort that certainly is not seen, but that can mean more than many meetings and passages of the law. Every Christian shall do his best so that the social machinery should function smoothly and in a manner that is not only formally correct but also helps people make it through their conflicts and difficulties.

Finally, the pastor is also a public servant. He is the population registrar and chairman of the church council; he often has a hand in childcare, school, or welfare, and sometimes all three.[6] The church makes social contributions here too. It is just one — not always known or recognized — fact that it is the priesthood that has built up the Swedish public school system. The hours of work that the pastors of three generations sacrificed to the building of schools, regulations, and rules of procedure, in teacher choice, in statistics, and in payroll requisition are incalculable. They often happened late in the evening and cost an infinite period of working overtime at protocols, tables, and cost estimates.

---

6 In Sweden, where there is a state church, the pastors have often been given these "clerical" duties. Indeed our own English word clerical and clerk are derived from the word clergy for these official roles that pastors have historically had in explicitly state church environments. However, though what is true of Sweden and other western European countries is not true in the same way for other contexts. Yet a case could be made that a pastor is a public servant regardless of official duties and has some responsibility for these things in the communities they represent, especially if they are asked to serve on a town council or a committee of some sort involving the community. It is not, nor does it necessarily have to be, in conflict with their duties as a pastor to preach the Gospel.

Now here arises a question that every pastor knows well. Does a *seelsorger* have time for that? Does he have a right to do that? Does not his pastoral work get drowned in the bottomless sea of statistics and numbers?

It has been asked what the priesthood was doing during this time when the new evangelism swept over large swaths of the land and in many cases robbed the churches of their best church people. There is at least an ounce of truth in the bitter answer: they were occupied up over their ears with carrying out the public school statute of 1842.

In any case it is a great injustice to accuse the priesthood of all too little social interest. Perhaps a person can have reason to speak about a one-sided or incorrectly focused interest. Perhaps a person can accuse the church of a fatal blindness to many of the social problems that grew up in connection with industrialization and the arrival of new railroad communities. However, it would be unjust to say that "the priesthood did nothing." The fact is that the majority of the priesthood worked an incredibly unfathomable amount for society, first and foremost in the creation of schools but also for the care of the poor and childcare. Not to speak of the pastors who supported almost the entire communal stewardship in their congregations. Rather, a person can ask if all this social work was fatal for our people because the pastors sometimes were more public servants than pastors, which in turn had its consequence in that the pastors did not have as much time for religious development.

The problem has a particular accentuation because the pastor's old Adam has a certain penchant for social work. In one respect it is an easy and convenient work: it can be done without faith. It belongs to that part of God's Word that can be fulfilled by blind instruments. A person does not need to be a man of prayer nor stand under God's guidance to build up a respectable school system. It can be a great temptation for a pastor for whom the flame of prayer and zealous fire of faith are about to be extinguished so that they have no real talent to tend to preaching, to gain respect or be cherished for their socially justifiable work despite their empty church. In other words, the pastor gathers compensation for his misfortune as a pastor by cutting his losses and working as a community organizer. A person can then say about the social work approximately what Paul says about the law: certainly, it is good and right and without a doubt comes from God, but through the strange power of sin it is still a source of death, both for the pastor and his congregation. The means of healing cannot be sought in that a person radically rejects all manifestations of the social duty. It can only be sought in a right use of both the pastoral office and the social duty. The pastor must first and foremost be a pastor. Yet he must also find a way to deal with as much of the social as may be his call. How the border should be drawn depends on a series of circumstances that vary from congregation to congregation. It depends on the congregation's size and on access to competent abilities. As a rule, the pastor ought to strive to put as much as possible on the shoulders of others. It is only beneficial for the community to share the work and responsibility as much as possible and to foster as many coworkers as possible in the administrative apparatus. But it can also happen that the pastor must take a task that he would rather avoid because there is in fact no one else that can manage it.

Now this applies to pastors and it is said mostly concerning the countryside. However, the problem is not only a pastoral problem. Laymen too can wrestle with the question of how they should find the strength and time to do their communal duty. For a farmer who stands without sufficient help on the farm, or a merchant who is already drowning in his forms and circulars—just as for many other dutiful men—for just this reason, for the unreasonably exploited laymen it means a real sacrifice to be able to take part in the social work. For them it goes approximately the same as I have just said with the pastor. A person may weigh and test the matter, laying it before God. A Christian does not avoid assessing whether it is perhaps just here God wants to see us serve our brother. Society has a limitless need of stewards and social workers who take their task seriously. The whole of this social legislation fails if there are not good, righteous men who translate the paragraphs into action. Just as the old church awakening created characters who, through their faithfulness, at the very least became a firm frame in society, Christendom today ought to be able to give our people faithful, enduring, and unpretentious coworkers in the social care that is needed if modern society should be successful in its praiseworthy striving to take care of the people. We have no right to bury our talent. It may cost prolonged days of work and still some hours wrestling with forms and the inconceivable constitutions. Finally, it still always means living men. It means letting them know the heart behind the paragraphs. It means giving the least among our brothers the personal consideration and the human treatment that allow them to understand that society is not a soulless machine of paper, proclamations, public servants, and stamps and lines, but a real communion where we all have responsibility for each other. Society shall be a servant of God for man's best interest. Thankfully, individuals who want to be God's servants receive new opportunities to take on our brother and do good for our fellow man. "And let us not grow weary of doing good, for in due season we will reap, if we do not give up" (Gal. 6:9).

THE FREEDOM OF THE CHURCH

When finally, after decades of prayer and struggle, Laurentius Petri was able to see the Swedish church order confirmed, he is said to have remarked that now he could depart in peace because he had been able to see the long-awaited day that confirmed the church's freedom — *quoniam optatam vidisset libertatis Ecclesiae diem.*

At that time, our first evangelical archbishop took to his lips the old and well-known slogan *libertas ecclesiae*. It has long been forgotten. Perhaps in our generation it will come to have a new ring. It stands for the values that we could not dispose of without the risk of losing the Gospel itself.

But what does the church's freedom mean? During the Middle Ages it was the slogan for a church politic that tended to subject all earthly authority to the church. Here even the Reformation meant a return to Scripture. In the Augsburg Confession, the evangelical view of the church's place in society is formulated. The church has no other authority than the spiritual, which she exercises by proclaiming the Gospel and administrating the sacraments. She has God's commission to preach repentance and the forgiveness of sins. However, she cannot force anyone to be a Christian. The church shall also not have any worldly power. Yet she shall have freedom to preach the Gospel and to shape her congregational life in accordance with God's Word. The state has no authority over her religious functions.

Translated into practical politics this means that the state with its laws shall not try to force anyone to be a Christian, but that it shall let God's Word be freely proclaimed so that everyone has opportunity to be a Christian.

A person cannot say that these principles were quite successfully actualized after the Reformation. Right at the beginning, state interest came to drive developments. The authority that the pope had in questions concerning external church direction was overtaken by the new national royal court. Gustav Vasa would like to have also annexed the spiritual powers and made the church into a department of the state. On this point a tough battle was fought for more than a half century until finally the church's vital rights were respected.[7] The church remains free in the essentials. The new church order, our Magna Carta, was received among the

---

7 Bo Giertz gives interesting insight into this battle in his novel *Faith Alone, The Heart of Everything*, which also weaves the other elements of Reformational theology spoken about here into the plot.

we reflect Kingdom of heaven, not world?

confessional writings and given binding character for the future. The bishops and the spiritual estate received responsibility for the proclamation of the Word, the pure teaching, and the proper administration of the sacraments. The congregations preserved their self-governance and so much of their property as was needed so that ecclesiastical activity would be able to continue. On the other hand, the king took control of the remaining church leadership so far as it applied to the worldly and administrative side. This was accepted by the church with the motivation that as a member of the church the king himself had God's commission to protect and promote the Gospel.

So, a modus vivendi had been found that has been preserved in principle to our day. The church is an institution beside the state with its own spiritual leaders, its own means of administration, its own taxation, its own congregational government, and its own influence in legislation. Its close relationship with the state is embodied in the king's person. He is the

we are all priests

church's worldly head, and as such according to the constitution, obligated to confess the pure evangelical teaching.

So, the Reformation had found an acceptable resolution. Under a Christian king the church has had free opportunity to proclaim the Gospel. Things went much worse with the principle of not forcing anyone in things that touched upon faith. The religious unity became a state interest of the very first order. Because during the Vasa era the papistry came to mean the same as treason, the state authority brought about absolute religious uniformity with a hard hand, and the church's men had it just too easy to find themselves corrected by state-directed religious coercion. Over nearly 300 years it became obvious that a Swede should be Lutheran.

The unity of our people's religion has long since been broken. Anyone who loves the pure Gospel has to mourn that this has happened. But at the same time, we have to be serious about our evangelical confession. The church does not have authority to force anyone. Above all she has God's great offer of the forgiveness of sins. If anyone will not receive this, then they cannot be coerced. Every form of ecclesiastical coercion is unevangelical.

Formally the Swedish state still maintains a religious coercion that ought to be unparalleled in any democratic land. A Swedish citizen is really obliged to belong to the Swedish Church so long as he does not announce his withdrawal to some other religious organization. For more than twenty years the church convention has demanded that this should be changed so that everyone who does not want to be a Christian should be free to leave the church. It looks as if this initiative should now lead to the result that free withdrawal will finally be a legal possibility.

With that a completely new situation enters our land that could hardly have any equivalent in history. We come to find a group of religion-less citizens who in any case ought to be free from paying the church tax, yet should not have any claim to influence the direction of the church. The church is thus an institution clearly distinguished from the state.

The question is now if the resolution of the relationship between the state and the church that the Reformation created comes to show itself to be durable. The situation has gradually shifted. What was before the evangelical king's personal concern for God's church has more and more become a function of the central administration. This in turn has been all the more secularized. Should this development continue, it must sooner or later come to a crisis.

Still, we only see this crisis as a possibility that would occur under unfortunate circumstances. Yet every evangelical Christian must make it clear for himself what is at stake. It simply must be recognized that if it were factually unreasonable in the future, the evangelical church's most vital questions should be possessed and handled by men who are not concerned with the Gospel and do not understand what the church serves. Here it does not mean more or less equal things, but real questions of

life that directly touch upon the ability to proclaim the Gospel. This means the existence of a
congregation, their sharing and mergers, opportunity to set up new clergy services in propor-
tion to an expanding population, appointment
of pastoral services, the Christian home's right
to prepare their children in an orderly confirmation instruction, and a lot of other things. To
hand over the decision in such questions to secularized people would be in fact as unreasonable as filling all the seats in the Royal Medical
Commission with chiropractors and homeo-
pathic practitioners, or to subject the defense
department to pacifists who do not believe in
defense. Yes, it would be still more unreasonable, for the defense system — and also partially
the care of the sick — is still state business, established and maintained by the means of the state,
but the church and her congregations have not
been established or paid for by the state. They
have arisen through Christian missions and
through the interest of Christian men to willingly sacrifice and cooperate with each other.

It is only a historical opportunity that gave the state co-influence over the administration of the church. The state has no moral right to use this influence to injure the church by hindering the activity of congregations or to take their possessions from them.

With a little goodwill, the question of the state's relationship to the church could be resolved in a manner that meets all reasonable demands for freedom of opinion and respect for the convictions of others. In Finland, these questions were regulated already in 1922 in a very congenial way that gives every citizen full freedom in religious views, and at the same time still respects the church's right to live according to her faith and confession. There is no reason why this question cannot be resolved along the same lines among us. The most important step in this direction is already being taken up with the implementation of free withdrawal.

While we wait for a good resolution in accord with tolerance and religious freedom, it is reasonable and just to demand that the state should not expand their power over the church. During the last few years there have been a couple opportunities for very expert opinions to assert that the state's power tends to gather new powers at the expense of the historic rights of the church and her congregations. Without needing to take a position on the critical points that apply here, it can be calmly asserted that such developments have less justification than ever before. In the interest of religious freedom, the church now agrees to separate from the state so that citizenship will no longer be the same as membership in the church. In this situation it is not reasonable that the church and her congregation's own organizations should be deprecated. It is just these bodies that a person must more and more come to trust for the church administration when the church can no longer include all people and the congregations no longer count as members the same as their community. It is not an expression for the pursuit of power, but for justice and sound reason if we on the side of the church just now assert our old rights, and we will not dispose of the freedom to govern our own church as we always have.

Should it go so far that it really affects the vital interests of our congregations, their right to live according to their confessions, their ability to maintain independence, the church's worship, her soul care, and her possessions, then it is necessary to resurrect the old banner with the slogan of the church's freedom. I am deeply convinced that this banner shall show itself to gather not only those for whom the evangelical faith of our fathers is a matter of the heart, but also those who have a deep-rooted love for our Swedish tradition of freedom.

EVANGELICAL FREEDOM

Finally, a word concerning evangelical freedom. It belongs to our reformational inheritance and may not be forgotten.

Evangelical freedom is not the same as laxity. Here the doctrine of justification by faith is the key to knowledge.

The Gospel is not just anything. It is the truth that everyone who believes in Jesus shall receive the forgiveness of sins through his name. Evangelical freedom is thus not freedom to believe whatever one wants.

Neither does this true faith in Jesus arise in any manner whatsoever. It is created by God through the Word and sacraments. An evangelical Christian is a biblical Christian and a Lord's Supper Christian. Evangelical freedom is not freedom to abandon one's congregation and devotions, nor freedom from prayer and church attendance.

True faith in Jesus does not show itself in just any way either. It is active in love, and this love shows itself first and foremost in good and honest vocational work. Evangelical freedom is thus not freedom to run away from daily duties to occupy oneself with some pious or impious work that suits itself better to the old Adam.

The evangelical church asserts all this in a manner and through the means with which she has been entrusted, without forcing anyone, but compelling with the power that lies in the Word, itself compelled by the love of Christ. If a person holds fast to this then a person can leave everything in peace that shall be left in peace. If there is evangelical firmness in the essentials, then there is also a place for evangelical freedom in adiaphora. If the foundation is correct, then there are many ways to build on it.

This applies first and foremost to worship. Lutherans have always been wide hearted in this matter. It has nothing against ceremonies if only they have evangelical content. They may not in any circumstance be made a basis of salvation. If they conflict with justification by faith or otherwise against holy Scripture, then no patina of age can save them. Yet if they have a clear evangelical meaning then they may be used freely. If they have come to us from the church of the old apostolic era, then we hold them in honor. It is the reformed with their legalistic view of worship and congregational order that have made a primary question concerning holy days, ornamentation, and altars. In the Lutheran Church we have gone a different way. We know that everything God has created is good when received with thanksgiving by those who believe. We know that God has created all colors, not just black. We can worship in spirit and truth in the ugliest of school halls, but when we have opportunity to adorn God's house, then we do it and say with the psalmist: "Lord, I love the habitation of your house, and the place where your glory dwells" (Psalms 26:8). We could very well celebrate the Lord's Supper around a wooden table, but when we have opportunity, we lay the table with all dignity and set a couple candles and a picture of the crucified Christ on it. We could very well receive gifts of the Lord's servant in drab dress, but we would rather come in churchly dress and adornment. If a man wants to clumsily point fingers at others for all this, we answer with the Augsburg Confession that "customs should be maintained that can be maintained without sin and which promote peace and good order in the church." If a man again makes a law of this and binds consciences, then we answer according to the same confession that "it is not necessary that the same statutes and church customs or humanly instituted ceremonies are found everywhere." "It is enough for the true unity of the church to agree concerning the teaching of the Gospel and the administration of the sacraments"(Kolb and Wengert, *Book of Concord*, art. VII, p. 43). We could allow one to have a little more and the other to have a little less of these forms through which the Word and sacraments are offered to us. It is a lack of sense for the essential if one begins to clamor about small things. Luther himself could commend the sign of the cross, and it was an obvious thing for him to bend the knee when he prayed in church. Such makes no one a papist or a Lutheran.

If the doctrine is right, then freedom can reign also in questions concerning the forms in which preaching clothes itself. Different tracts have different traditions. They may look at each other with brotherly tolerance. If Christ is rightly proclaimed and both law and gospel are spoken in the sermon that is orderly prepared, then it means nothing if the one has an outline and the other memorized while the third reads from the page. The pastor shall here follow the apostles' certain counsel to go after that which creates peace and edification in the congregation, and the congregation shall remember that no external manners could determine our place with God.

Freedom shall also reign when it comes to external forms for everyday life. In questions of customs and traditions, food and drink, clothing, and company a Christian is free. He shall show responsibility for his work and consideration for his family. He shall seek his neighbor's best interest like his own and try not to give a bad example for his weak brother. He shall live in prayerful association with God, hold fast to the means of grace, and test himself by the Word so that nothing may force its way between his heart and the Savior. When he settles all this, then he is free to form his life, his friends, his free time, his refreshment, his manner of dress, and his associations that he finds he can defend before God according to the Word. It is also just as bad with human statutes that make a law from that which God has left free, and which essentially say: You can't taste that, and you shall not do that, or you should not dress that way. This even applies to things of which Scripture says are destined for use in this world to be received with thanksgiving, and then pass away. "For freedom Christ has set us free; stand firm therefore, and do not submit again to a yoke of slavery" (Gal. 5:1).

In popular histories of the Reformation,[8] the foundational thoughts of the Reformation are presented in the following manner: Luther could not find a single word in his Bible saying that "God placed any value in penitential practices and other purely external works. On

---

8 Here Bo Giertz talks about how the Reformation is presented in Swedish public schools specifically.

the contrary, he found that 'God looks to the heart' and that this depends upon a state of mind whether or not a so-called good work has any value before the Almighty." Then it is said that according to Luther justification is to come through "faith in God as the good Father."

Factually seen, this is approximately just as absurd as saying that Luther fell at Fredrikshald,[9] or that he was the one who invented the art of penance. For Luther, that the Lord looks at a person's heart was not gospel at all. What he learned from both experience and Scripture was precisely that it is just the heart and state of mind of man that are so entangled by sin that not a single work is pure before the Almighty. In this distress no faith in God as the good Father was of any help. There needed to be a savior who bore his brother's guilt and allowed them to share his righteousness.

---

9 A siege for the city of Fredriksten in Norway (1718) at which King Charles XII died when hit in the head by a large projectile from the Norwegian defenders. This ended the Swedish era of imperialism.

It ought to give us pause that such a coarse factual mistake could appear in a textbook authored by one of our best-read historians. The inheritance of the Reformation could hardly be rightly administered in a land where such a thing can happen. In wide circles our "Lutheran" people are just as unknowledgeable about justification by faith as anyone in the day of Olaus Petri. We may start from the beginning again and not shy away from any effort to teach our fellow man the truth that is the key to all knowledge of salvation.

The task has never been easy and never will be. The message of the Reformation includes the very deepest in Christendom, that which can never be fathomed by reason before God himself moves upon the heart of a man. Here the Savior's word applies: God has "hidden these things from the wise and understanding but revealed them to little children" (Matt. 11:25). Here again we are placed before the truth that there is only one possibility for the church to remain: to trust in the power of the Lord's Word, to speak what he has given us to speak, assured that nothing is impossible for God.

INHERITANCE FROM THE AWAKENINGS

The great church awakenings[10] essentially taught us nothing new. They taught us a new application of that which the evangelical church always knew. The key of knowledge was found again. Now it was seriously placed in the lock, and the gates opened themselves to a new event in the history of our church. Great *seelsorgers* showed the way, and zealous disciples brought their teachings out to the villages. The inheritance of the Reformation was deepened

---

10 The great awakenings of which Bo Giertz speaks here should not be confused with the great awakenings that happened in America under men like Jonathan Edwards, Wesley, or Finney. Though the time period was largely the same, and there is crossover in some subject matter and at times even overlapping relationships, Bo Giertz is speaking of events in Sweden that had their own intricacies. Some of the larger names in the Swedish context would be Schartau and Rosenius.

and in best meaning made popular. The Gospel was as never before the common man's possession, experienced and understood in its deepest sense. It transformed customs and home. It gave our people a measure of Christian knowledge that went far beyond what any past generation had managed to give us.

The situation was in a certain way different than in Luther's day. Luther had rediscovered the Gospel during his desperate attempt to be righteous through works of the law. He had been a comforter and a liberator for all who failed under the same yoke. The Gospel of the forgiveness of sins for Christ's sake became the great discovery that caused people to open their eyes wide. They had found the pearl of great price, and they willingly invested everything in order to possess it.

Perhaps three hundred years later the pearl has lost some of its luster. Or more correctly, the eyes that would look at it had gone dim. The joyous news became old. Since childhood people had learned to expect to hear that we are justified by pure grace. It was an obvious truth, without power to awaken sympathy in the heart that had never been wounded by the sting of the law, and never knew any reason to fear God's wrath. The impenitently secure knew all too well what they would answer when the Word came with its demand for repentance and new life. They had learned to forge the doctrine of justification by faith into a suit of armor in which the old Adam could thump his chest, filled with the satisfaction of never needing to be anything but a poor sinner.

So, it was a vital necessity for the church to mark the difference between living faith and dead faith, between the real state of grace and the imagined. It became necessary to be able to preach this so vividly and clearly that an individual could recognize himself and test his position.

It is this problem that the men of the church awakenings wrestled with. So, they began to preach in a way that "made a difference with the people," and held up Bible stories that honestly and clearly drew up the boundaries between the unrepentant and salvation-seeking souls. So, they also awakened new life in the individual care of souls and introduced a confirmation instruction that was epoch making both in pedagogical clarity and serious soul care. They strongly taught both old and young concerning the essence of faith, of the true repentance, concerning signs of remorse, and about false foundations of comfort, all with a clarity that inexorably disclosed spiritual cheating and at the same time offered important help to see that grace applied just for them.

All this created a Lutheran and church awakening piety that can vary from village to village and from district to district, but which has very noticeable characteristics everywhere thatit influenced the life of the people, and where there are clearly drawn boundaries, both against the worldly affections and against false faith.

The first of these characteristics is a consciousness that something must happen with men. If a man has fallen away from God, then he must be brought back through a true conversion. Because most men had broken their baptismal covenant and given up their childhood God, there must be a change with them that makes it so that they could speak of a before and now, of a transition from death to life. Lutheran revival Christianity is thus thoroughly conversion Christianity.

The next sign is the clear insight that the conversion is a work of God that happens through the Word. The Word has a "heart-breaking power," a Spirit-given ability to work on us sinners. So, a conversion remains not only in that the man receives a new insight that overcomes his doubt or that he receives some decision of the will concerning a changed way of life. This consists of God's Word—both law and gospel—that penetrates a heart deeply, exposes its innermost abomination and at the same time lets it perceive that it is enveloped by God's love and Christ's death so that his righteousness is cast over all these sins. This work usually demands considerable time. The Word breaks down piece after piece of human self-consciousness and takes from him that which he by nature would rather build on in place of receiving the merits of Jesus: the first joy, the easy victories, warmth in prayer life. The last is that God's Spirit discloses false refuges, normally something like satisfaction concerning a person's own repentance or the faith they have in their own faith.

Schartau has given us the classical conclusion of all this in his instruction on the order of grace (*ordo salutis*). Yet this teaching is directly contrary to that which it is sometimes considered to be. In typical conformity with a doctrine of works, the skewed view tends conceive of the order of grace as a teaching about the soul's way to God through a series of reforms and purifications. What the order of grace really describes is the complete opposite, how God's Spirit discloses man's total inability to convert himself, to honestly love God and altruistically serve his neighbor. Just so he helps a man come forward to the Redeemer who alone can save him. Seen

most deeply, the order of grace is a teaching
about faith, not a description of stages that man
must go through in order to be a true Christian.
It is a description of all the obstacles in the heart
of man that arise on the way of faith, and of the
work through which God's Spirit broke them
down. What is essential in the order of grace
then is not the order but the grace. Here there
is certainly a connection that often appears in
a particular sequence of time, but the old doctrine had never made a sequence of time into a
law. They have certainly seen that a man must
be called and awakened so that he is carried to
a serious use of God's Word before there can
be any lasting result of the Spirit's work in his
heart. They have seen that he must be exposed
by law and gospel so that he learns to recognize his sins, his inner sinful inheritance, and
his Savior's work of redemption to be able to
come to faith. However, they have never meant
or said that this shall be able to be distinguished
as in "stages" or steps in a clearly staked path.
Everything intervenes in every other, and that

which once happened comes back in a new way and with new relationships. Only one thing is essential: that God himself may work through his Word, so that repentance is true, and the sinner comes to faith in Jesus alone.

This is the church awakening's third characteristic: concern that faith shall be true. With a clear perceptivity that is both strict and loving, it sees through all cheating when it comes to faith. It is not willing to equate grasping with faith or zeal with conversion. It very well knows that the Jews who were "zealous for God" still did not find salvation so long as they sought "to come accomplished in their own righteousness." Awakening knows that he who wants to be righteous by the power of the law falls from grace. It sees that it is just this striving that lies behind so much activity in modern spirituality and so much talk about the life, witness, and personal effort that are essential in Christendom. Awakening is suspicious of every speech about being converted by "giving your heart to God," "deciding for God," or "resolving to be a Christian." Concerning all this it can say that it is good and useful and necessary — but it is not conversion. In the best case this means that a man is a disciple and strikes upon the right path. The fathers called this "being awakened," to "be a seeking man," or to "come to consideration." Then it remains to learn something that is both more important and harder. A man can well enough "determine to be a Christian," but no such resolution is sufficient to kill the heathen within us. A man can well enough "give his heart to God" but then the question remains as to what God should do with such a lousy, worm-eaten thing. A man can well enough "make a decision for God," but it would almost be blasphemy to do it if God had not decided for us by giving his only begotten Son for us all. An awakened man learns all this if he obediently allows himself to be instructed. Yet it is both dangerous and wrong to call the awakened saved or converted and let them believe that their human ambition is the same as the Spirit's new life, to let them stand and testify to their own conversion and possibly make them leaders for a Christian function. Such often leads people to a point where, after a period of time, they are disappointed with everything and say that the whole of Christianity is humbug. They have begun to understand how human everything was, how little protection they had from all the great words and how fundamentally unchanged their heart is underneath it all. Yet instead of bowing deeper in the confessions of sins and the insight of their impotence, they blame Christianity and say that it does not keep what it promises. This is one of the dangers of false teaching.

Another danger is the complacent superficiality that really believes that a total change has happened because a man enthusiastically participates in new activities and answers the demand that is placed on a Christian's external way of life. In such a way a man can be an active associate and an interested parishioner, full of initiative, admired by his friends and yet find talk of the heart's hopeless corruption to be perfectly incomprehensible. It is the fine form of Pharisaism that in its rock-solid conviction and zealousness for God constitutes the greatest hindrance for a true conversion.

The fourth of the church awakening's characteristics is the energetic emphasis on daily repentance. Conversion can never be a one-time thing for Lutherans. A man never grows out of the confession of sins. God's Word does not leave sin in peace. A long-tested Christian does not need less, but more forgiveness of sins and atoning grace. He lives in the daily conversion. His conscience is sensitive to the Word's slightest rebukes. He means it seriously when he says that he is a great sinner. So, he constantly takes new refuge in his Savior. He is always more deeply assured that he cannot be without him, and he constantly receives with renewed wonder the experience that the Savior has new forgiveness to give.

It is this ongoing work that shows that there is spiritual life in a man. Within the church awakening a man therefore does not gladly base his assurance that he is a child of God on something that one experiences or undergoes in the past. Instead, a man holds fast to the Word and prays to God that he who has begun a good work will also complete it before the day of Jesus Christ.

***

In the church awakening a man perceives the warm beat of the Lutheran heart. Here a man encounters in real life what otherwise so easily becomes a principle and theory. Academic Lutheranism is sometimes accused of being an unfruitful, quarrelsome condition. Where awakening works, Lutheranism has borne fruit. This principle has vividly stepped forth in the form of restored stolen goods, repaid money, fulfilled promises, and scrupulously fulfilled everyday work. Its insignia has been home devotions, worn Bibles, and huge crowds in the churches listening with attention, devotion, and a perceptual ability before which even an uncomprehending stranger sometimes feels strangely caught.

Should our church be unfaithful to this inheritance of the awakening she would deny her own Lord and his most obvious works. It would be foolish to believe that our generation with its weak spiritual resources would be able to strike a line through all that is the fruit of countless Christian lives and gifted works of teaching, filled with the study of Scripture, prayer, and care for souls. It does not help that a man cites Luther to undermine the church awakenings. The church awakening is not the fruit of a theoretical Luther study. It is a living Lutheranism, translated into everyday life, a Lutheranism that in life and death fights with all the enemies of the Gospel all around us and in our own hearts. A man can never understand it and judge it right if he does not take into account all the developments after Luther and all that which God taught us in our church since the 1500s.

What seems most challenging in the inheritance from the awakening is obviously the assertion that there is something that is called revival, and that not all religious zeal or every serious decision means a true faith. To our human nature it is just so intolerable that we could not be able to believe in Jesus even if we really and honestly want to. For the awakened who expect to be gratefully accepted without further ado, it is shocking to hear that he must again reconsider his spiritual foundations. For a pastor who himself lacks the sense for differences between legalist zeal and living faith, it is unbearable to hear that just this distinction is fundamental in true preaching and true soul care.

So here the critique sets in. A man says that the Bible has nothing to say about the order of grace or revival. It is just as justified to say that neither does it talk about three persons in the divinity, or about faithfulness in the call. The terms are lacking. They are created by Christian thinkers working with the biblical text. However, the subject matter is there.

An observant Bible reader quickly finds that not all "faith" in the New Testament is the same as that which we call saving faith. In John 18, Jesus speaks "to the Jews who believed in him." He instructs them precisely, saying that they must remain in his word in order to be true disciples. Only then will they understand the truth and the truth will set them free from their bondage to sin.

From the whole New Testament, it appears clear that true faith is the faith that causes men who do not trust in any sort of spiritual asset of their own to take their refuge in Jesus Christ, "whom God put forward as a propitiation" (Rom. 3:25). Yet it appears just as clearly that this faith can be lacking in the midst of the Christian congregation. The classical example is Galatians, where Paul so sharply rebukes the Galatians because they began to gaze at the law and wanted to trust in it as the path of salvation. He says right out that they have fallen from grace and away from Christ because they now want to be justified by the power of the law. But he does not exclude them. He admonishes and warns them. He makes it clear to them that the entirety of ourselves is encompassed under sin, and he points to Christ who redeemed us from the curse of the law.

This is the church's way. We know very well that faith is not true so long as there is a secret or open trust in our own merits. Now the church's task is to let the Word work a true faith. The disciples are all who hear the Word and receive it with sincere hearts. So, the church does not need to test the faith of an individual. She does not hold examinations of faith as a condition for access to her sanctuaries or the Lord's Supper. Everyone who wants to take the path of discipleship and follow his master to be instructed, he is welcome. Yet for all this, the church preaches seriously and penetratingly about sin and grace, about the heart's corruption and Christ's atonement, about the contrast between self-righteousness and God's righteousness. Then she crushes all false supports of faith and anchors faith where it shall be anchored, on Christ the rock.

Natural reason takes all this unnecessarily hard. It would be much simpler to say that either one has faith, or one does not have faith. They who do not have faith do not seek Jesus. However, those who seek him, they must have faith — naturally insofar as they are not hypocrites. Everyone is agreed that there are imposters. They are like Judas and Ananias, and sooner or later they are destroyed.

This could be rightly reasoned if really all pharisees were imposters and all honest striving was of faith. But in actual fact, human hearts firmly cling with an obvious inclination to the law's false path of salvation. Pharisaism is not finished because man asserts that he believes in Christ. Even when a man comes to Jesus and follows him, there remain deeply rooted cravings to "accomplish one's own righteousness." This self-righteousness is a hindrance for salvation, just as serious as any promiscuity or blasphemy. It belongs to the most urgent and hardest tasks of soul care to get such zealous disciples to understand that the most important things can be lacking even in them. They are themselves convinced of the sincerity of their faith. They are completely convinced that they want to belong to Christ and serve him. If this means the same as Luther said about his time in the monastery, "all that I did, I did in sincere zealousness and for God's sake."

Now it is very peculiar to see two pages later in the same book what Luther says about the very same period in his life: "in the midst of all this holiness and self-reliance I fed a constant distrust and was full of doubt, despair, hate, and blasphemy before God." This can sound like a complete contradiction. In actual fact it gives an appropriate picture of the duality in a man who has a legalistic faith in Christ. He is no imposter. He can honestly say that he believes in his Lord and holds fast to him. However, a deeper look shows this is hypocrisy. The whole of his will is set in that he should accomplish something that counts before God. He has found a program for life and an activity that he enters into with all his energy. He knows what Christ wants, and he is convinced that he shall be able to carry it through with his help. He is also convinced that his right to be called a Christian now means successfully completing this program. This creates a warp in his relationship to both God and man. If he thinks he is successful, he records his progress as an asset before God, and also gladly makes it into a platform from which he looks down on other men. If it goes badly, a secret distress grows within him that will eventually lay the blame on the Gospel or on God himself.

It is this that gives even the most sincere piety of the law a draft of falseness. All this remains hidden to a slave of the law until God has revealed and condemned even this innermost enmity toward God and established the faith that counts all his own for refuse and will not boast of anything but the cross of Christ. If God's Spirit can open the eyes so that a man sees this, then a man like Luther may also see that what is seen from man's side as honest zeal is before God a selfish love and hidden hate of Christ's cross.

So long as this falseness rules the soul, faith cannot be right. So long may man also count that everything can end in catastrophe. When it goes forward with this supposed sanctification, when the hearing of prayer is absent, when despite all his working a man is not accepted without further ado by some old Christians, when a man may not vent his desire to govern and fix and play a role, then the old Adam rises up and declares perhaps one day that now he is altogether tired. Or he continues stubbornly and belligerently on his own way and makes a virtue and a chief truth of just that which meets with the sharpest of criticism.

This catastrophe with discipleship can only be averted by a catastrophe for the old man. The awakened soul must make the same discovery as Luther in the monastery, or Paul on the road to Damascus: that all this has been a form of egoism and self-assertion before God. All this that before was gain, is then a loss. Yet the Gospel about atonement, that a person listened to before out of obligation but fundamentally regarded as a little boring and completely unnecessary, it is now life's bread and the soul's source of joy.

When it comes to tutoring such men, we have much to learn from the church awakening—first and foremost the certain mercy that lies in the tripart division. Should one divide men into converted and unconverted, then these seeking men would be unconverted without any further consideration. Yet now there is also such as those who stand before conversion, and they are real disciples even now. A person can encounter them with confidence and encouragement and let them know that they are on the way. Even if the one thing necessary is still lacking with them, so they have then gone looking for it. A person can then take them by the hand and feel belonging with them as disciples feel with each other. Yet a person should not tell them that everything is okay with their faith. A man tells them that it is a great joy that they have begun to listen attentively to the Word because the Word has so incredibly much to say that we do not understand at the beginning. He lets them understand that they perhaps still have the best and most important learning remaining. He reminds them that the deep insight in the Word is not gained in a couple evenings but is a fruit of a fundamental work of the Spirit in the soul. He admonishes them to not believe that they understand everything or that God is finished with them. And first and last he asks them to faithfully continue to give attention to the Word and bow to its discipline.

There is something quite merciful in this basic view, something that separates our church awakening inheritance from other types of revival. It is not a question of pushing forth some precocious result. A person has time to wait. All rests in the secure certainty: God works here. If the Word is merely proclaimed and rightly received, then the fruit cannot stay away.

This security belongs to the sort in the inheritance of the awakening that we ought to take special care with. The church is God's work. God has put the means of salvation into our hands. If we use them then something happens, in his time and in his way. Lutheran piety is not orderly, not rushed and plagued by the thought that it is we who must do it. Yet neither is it idle. The "lazy Lutheranism" is no true Lutheranism, but an apostasy, a form of unbelief. True evangelical piety is the art of being both active and secure, to do your best within your call and then calmly wait for the growth from God.

So, the evangelical faith lives in this world, and the awakening is passed on from generation to generation. The children are brought to baptism. The mothers teach them to pray, teach them the basics of God's Word at the same time they teach them their mother tongue. Of all life's tasks this is one of the greatest, the most filled with responsibility and most fruitful: to teach a child to know the Lord Jesus at whose command they were baptized. Then the work continues through church attendance and Sunday school, in Christian instruction and confirmation. Everything has its time and demands its effort at prayer and work. If it goes as it should, the young grow in the circles of the fathers by listening and celebrating the Lord's Supper.

This does not mean that awakening and conversion stay away. In the same manner as an awakened man learns to know his sinful corruption, and so as the believing soul in new situations encounters new temptations and new hindrances that only God's Spirit can break down, so a young Christian encounters on his way the old difficulties, and experiences anew what the fathers before us went through. The result is the same overall; we decrease, and he increases. The heart's love and longing gather all the more around this one thing: to participate in his salvation and his power of resurrection.

That this whole time has dealt with the question of awakening, it shows therein that the question of salvation is personally burning, so it is also individual soul care. A person needs counsel and seeks help from his *seelsorger*. There is also consideration of others. There is a mother and a father's most burning anxiety, that the child shall find a good Christian education, that they should take their confirmation seriously and choose a way of life that does not take them away from Christ. The master of the house feels responsibility for the people of his home, and also thinks of their opportunities to go to church. Neighbors help both when it comes to everyday worries and going to church. And if any go astray in lost ways, then he is followed by the prayers of others and is never alone, never completely abandoned by the good powers that God's Word woke to life in the village.

CONCLUSION

I have again spoken with the countryside before my eyes. It is there that the church in the past has harvested the richest harvest for eternity. A new time has come with new problems, conditioned by the seemingly irresistible growth of great cities. Long has the church stood reasonably handcuffed before this development. A frozen organization that made congregational distribution into a concern of the state has paralyzed her adaptability. Here we expect our most mandatory tasks. We have no reason to despair. Early Christendom showed its power to overcome the world first and foremost in great cities. The Christ who worked then is the same today. The crucified has died also for the tens of thousands on the edges of the great city that are now so often left without spiritual care. The Resurrected One also walks around among the new rows of houses where it can sometimes seem as if no one knows him. It is no more unreasonable that here should grow forth living congregations than that Rome and Corinth once became Christian.

This awakening that is needed here must perhaps find a form that externally separates itself from the classical church awakening out in our villages. And yet its content, its power, and its Christian content must be gathered from the church awakening's old springs. Here it means to teach in the right manner, both clearly and humbly. We do not learn from the past in order to conserve what men thought and did. Human traditions may never be so dear to us. We can still dispense with them. What we cannot dispense with is God's own work, the Word's work in our hearts. The right manner of learning from the fathers is to open oneself for the work that God carried out during the time of awakening.

If the Word is able to work in our own hearts, so that we ourselves live by the old message and understand the old Word about sinful corruption and atonement, then—and only then—have we the opportunity to carry the work further. Then we can understand why the fathers worked just as they did. Then we could hope to actually find the right means and the boldness to go further, certain that the Resurrected One himself shall show us the way.

So, we have again come back to the starting point. "If Christ has not been raised, then our preaching is in vain and your faith is in vain . . . But in fact Christ has been raised from the dead" (1 Cor. 15:14 and 20). If we deny him then he shall deny us. If we do not believe in his Word then all power leaves us. But if we stand fast to his Word, then the Lord who triumphs over the dead and all powers of the abyss is at work. Then what he said to one of his first congregations also applies to us: "Behold, I have set before you an open door, which no one is able to shut. I know that you have but little power, and yet you have kept my Word and have not denied my name" (Rev. 3:8).

———◈———

This greeting I have sent to the ministerium and congregations of the diocese I have necessarily produced under a busy and pressing time. The short weeks that were available have been so filled with new duties that there has not been much time for the research and editing I would have liked. I dare to confess that on more than one occasion I have been tempted to throw the pen from my hand and say this is impossible. It will never do.

I know that I am not alone with this. That tasks pile up, that there is insufficient time, this has been a very common experience for our generation. This is true for both pastors and laymen, both professional work and duties in the home. We are all pressed at times to work under conditions that could seem impossibly hard and unfavorable. We are placed before tasks where we know that our strength is not sufficient. We are tempted to push everything away from us. Like your employees you are also placed under the same demands, and I send a greeting and an admonition to you all who work in Christ's church within the Gothenburg diocese. This may now happen in the service of the Word or in the diaconate, as cantors or church servants, or in some of the civil duties where the church's living members see their Lord. I pray you all to work further, persistently and faithfully. We may be thankful for every task where God lets us do something for some fellow man. We may not always demand ideal working conditions that guarantee us the best conceivable results. We may be satisfied that day after day God gives us the possibility to serve. We may humble ourselves and not keep ourselves from doing good workwhere both we and others can see the need. Tribulation and adversity come to encounter us, perhaps even thanklessness and suffering. Let us calmly keep on and every day do our best. The essential thing is that we do not lose the sources of strength and the comfort that God gives to every little lamb in his church. Concerning them I have tried to speak in this letter. I admonish each and every one of them to cultivate and nurture. In them lies the mysterious content that makes it possible for us to be born again to a living hope so that we endure the difficulties of he who has borne all the tribulation of human life, overcame its temptations, and atoned for his brother's missteps. To him belongs the glory. Amen.

So, I sign this letter with an apostolic word from the last book of the Bible which expresses just that which I most of all wish for you.

Your brother with you has a share in the sorrow and the kingdom and the steadfastness in Jesus.

Gothenburg in the cathedral, 8th June 1949

CPSIA information can be obtained
at www.ICGtesting.com
Printed in the USA
LVHW012355100422
715851LV00003B/183